Burntwater

Scott

Thybony

BURNTWATER

The

University

of Arizona

Press

Tucson

The University of Arizona Press

© 1997 The Arizona Board of Regents

♾ This book is printed on acid-free, archival-quality
paper

Manufactured in the United States of America

02 01 00 99 98 97 6 5 4 3 2 1

Library of Congress Cataloging-in-Publication Data

Thybony, Scott.

Burntwater / Scott Thybony.

p.   cm.

ISBN 0-8165-1456-9 (cloth : alk. paper). —

ISBN 0-8165-1480-1 (pbk. : alk. paper)

1. Four Corners Region—Description and travel.

2. Four Corners Region—Biography—Anecdotes.

3. Indians of North America—Four Corners

Region.—Anecdotes.   4. Thybony, Scott—

Journeys—Four Corners Region.   I. Title.

F788.5.T49   1997

979.2'59—dc21   96-45807

CIP

British Cataloguing-in-Publication Data

A catalogue record for this book is available from the
British Library.

Publication of this book is made possible in part by
the proceeds of a permanent endowment created with
the assistance of a Challenge Grant from the National
Endowment for the Humanities, a federal agency.

Contents

Preface   vii

Deeper In   1

Mad Kelly   7

Sun Chief   11

The Singer   21

Redwall   35

No Man   45

Blind Trail   55

Roadman   67

Encircled Mountain   73

Brothers of Light   81

Stone Lions   95

Under the Rim   103

Returning   115

Preface

Outside the ranch house, the dogs are barking at the shadow of a coyote moving across the field. The dark bulk of the San Francisco Mountains pushes above the trees as pale light lifts along the eastern skyline.

This is home, a mile below the mountain summit and a mile above the canyon floor, the point of balance. This is where my wife and son lie dreaming. I'm waiting for them to wake up, waiting for enough light to pack the truck and go. No matter how many times I sit here before a trip, the excitement builds.

Certain places take us beyond ourselves. The Four Corners country is one of them. The long distances tug at the soul, drawing us far beyond the familiar. A friend once stopped at a bar in Bluff, Utah, for a gin-and-tonic before leaving on a river trip. The bartender looked straight at him. "This is the edge of America," she said. "Have a beer."

Years ago I unfolded a road map and found a place on the Navajo reservation called Burntwater. I wasn't sure what was there, maybe a trading post and a waterhole with a story. But the name fit this country. I drew a circle around it, planning to head there someday. With most of my traveling tied to my work as a writer, Burntwater remained just another name on a list of possibilities. Then a postponed deadline opened up a couple of weeks, giving me the chance to take a trip out of simple curiosity.

An old friend, Scott Milzer, signed on. He had some discretionary time before joining his fishing boat in Alaska. When he arrived in Flagstaff, we pulled out the topos and plotted a rough course around the Four Corners. We decided to take the long way, following the backroads where the ruins outnumber the ranches and the locals still wave to strangers. Early spring weather would add an element of surprise to the trip, but it also meant empty roads and emptier backcountry.

Our plan was to cross the Colorado Plateau, entering places layered with history and legend, places unfamiliar to us. We wanted to cover the land between the headwaters of the Virgin River and the mouth of the Dirty Devil, running between Mollies Nipple and Cads Crotch, passing from the Blue Desert to the Red. We wanted to string together towns with names like Mexican Hat and Shiprock. Leaving Flagstaff, we planned to head north into the raw beauty of southern Utah, following a long arc into New Mexico before swinging back to Arizona.

Nothing was locked in. With the weather only one of the uncertainties, we needed flexibility. We loaded the truck with backpacking gear, food and water, a climbing rope, a widow-maker jack, and whatever else we might need for a bivouac or a breakdown. My friend even threw in his ocean-survival suit. We were ready. So from a name, we took a direction; with the direction came a beginning. The rest followed.

All people within these pages are real; the events happened; the places exist. The Four Corners region, labeled as Indian Country on some maps, provides the setting. But what I have to say about the Navajo and Hopi reveals more about myself than them. They speak for themselves. For narrative purposes, the organization of chapters veers away from strict chronological order. And, of course, much of what happened doesn't appear in the story. To write is to choose. I've selected what matters to me. Others would choose differently.

Once I made a trip to Lukachukai with a friend, John Farella. Both of us wrote up our notes afterward and traded copies. They were completely different; not a single incident turned up in both sets of notes. What he found of interest, I ignored. What I focused on, he overlooked. But in each, the people were recognizable and the places familiar. All the particulars differed, but the pattern held.

A writer incurs debts he can recognize but not repay. My thanks to Sandy, who reads everything, who gets the first taste and lets me know when it still needs to simmer; to Erik who never complains when I return from somewhere bringing back another strange rock; to fellow travelers Scott Milzer, Tony Williams, John Farella, Terry Gustafson, and the others who were there; and to those living in pueblo, hogan, double-wide, and adobe—the ones who took the risk of talking to a writer without knowing how the words would fall onto the page, the ones who keep reminding me life is more than the evening news.

Daylight grows stronger; the shape of the world emerges again. Time to begin.

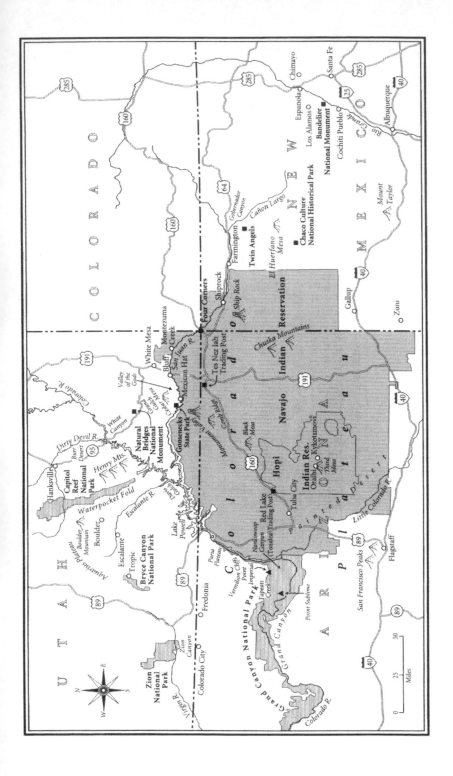

Deeper In

A narrow track draws us north through slickrock domes and a scatter of trees. Farther west the leading edge of a storm sweeps across a dark divide. I watch the bank of stormclouds overtake us as pockets of deep sand slow our forward movement. Momentum is all that counts, and maybe a little luck. That's the way it's always been.

Another warning sign appears with the same message as one we already passed. My friend Scott Milzer reads it out loud as a reminder, "4-Wheel Drive Only."

Swinging the two-wheel-drive pickup into a curve, I head deeper into the Sand Hills toward the far rim of Paria Plateau. At 6,000 feet in elevation, the March air has a bite to it. The road dips and rolls as we cover the first leg of a trip through the Four Corners country. Milzer unfolds a map and scans the region where the borders of Arizona, Utah, Colorado, and New Mexico meet in a geographic transept.

A few hours before, we left Flagstaff without a final destination in mind, only a direction. We are heading toward a place called Burntwater in the Navajo country. But the name no longer appears on newer maps. We are heading toward a place that might not exist, one that has fallen off the map and left a blank spot where it used to be. Where we end up, we'll leave to chance.

Clouds lower and the air thickens, cutting us off from all landmarks. The two of us drift untethered across the plateau as the collapsing weather buries the road ahead. A juniper twists out of the blank expanse and quickly fades back; a rocky outcrop floats above the surface and subsides behind us. We follow a blind trackway toward a place neither of us has seen before.

As snow begins to fall, the gray half-light absorbs all depth, making it hard to tell if the road is climbing or dropping. I angle the truck down two ruts in the sand, hoping to reach the edge of the plateau somewhere beyond.

Suddenly I hit the brakes. The slope in front pitches sharply downward to the floor of a deep draw. If we keep going, the truck will never make it back up. I put it into reverse and give it a touch of gas. The rear wheels spin in the loose sand, and I ease off the accelerator to keep from digging in. We sit there a moment studying the situation, neither of us surprised.

I climb out to check the slope behind us. It's sandy but not too steep. With a little work we might have a chance to back out the way we came. Grabbing a shovel stowed in the back, I begin digging as Milzer places boards behind each wheel.

When everything is ready, he pushes from the front as I steer. The engine whirs higher in pitch with each rev; the truck rocks onto the boards. Looking back I see a wisp of smoke drift from a pinwheeling tire. No traction. I turn the key off and step into the deep quiet. It will take a full day of digging, laying brush, and pushing to get back to the top of the ridge — either that or go forward.

We walk down the slope, splitting up to increase our chances of finding another way out. The terrain has closed in as tightly as the weather. Crossing the draw to the far side, I see only more sand and steeper slopes. Somewhere to the north, Buckskin Gulch cuts a slot through the plateau, joining the storm-covered Paria gorge beyond. Far to the south, the great barrier cliffs of the Grand Canyon drop into their own weather.

As I turn back, snow begins to fall more heavily, bringing with it an early dusk. The line between sky and earth thins. Rock dissolves into air. From somewhere above comes a raven's cry, pitched on the edge between memory and thought. A dark wing passes overhead, dips, and circles back. Wherever I go, the bird is there. A presence. It lifts above the broken cliffs, missing nothing.

Another cry, and a second shape appears, as black as a hole punched in the sky. The two ravens reel upward, disappearing into an endless field of falling snow. As I stare above, I feel a peculiar reversal of motion, a retrograde shift. The snow hangs suspended for a moment, and the earth rises upward.

Scott calls, too far away for me to understand him. I turn back and walk toward his voice. On each side of the draw, a coating of snow softens the edges of the terrain.

"There's a cabin down there and an old road heading up the ridge," he tells me when I catch up with him. "It doesn't look as steep as the one we're on."

Figuring it's our best chance, we return to the truck. I put it in gear and press the accelerator. Sometimes the only way out is deeper in.

The truck barrels down the drop, sand flying. Once on the bottom of the ravine, I keep the pickup moving until reaching a solid patch of slickrock next to the line camp. The old road looks passable as far as I can see, but a stand of trees screens most of it from view.

"Let's walk it out," I say.

We haven't gone far before the road curves into a tight bend of soft, deeply rutted sand. Inspecting it carefully, we check different approaches but know the pickup won't make it through. It will bog down as it rounds the turn, if it doesn't high-center first. The road is out.

We find ourselves caught within a pattern of weather and terrain, deep in a far corner of the country, west by southwest, in a place as different as you can find and still call it America.

Unsure what to do, we walk toward the abandoned cabin, needing time to think. I half-expect to see smoke rising from the chimney or a light shining from the window. The mind is willing to face anything but emptiness. Look at a blank spot on the map and it soon fills with lost rivers and legendary mountains.

"It's a cowboy's Christmas," Milzer says, as we approach the snow-covered shack. Pushing open a broken screen door, we enter the front room. A scurrying comes from the walls as something hurries away unseen, claws scratching across rough-cut boards. A wren's nest sits empty on a shelf; a cold woodstove takes up the corner.

Tacked next to the door, a photograph shows an expanse of dead hills, windless and untouched by rain. Standing in a deserted cabin among the sand hills, I stare at an image of the ultimate desert, a photo taken on the far side of the moon. The first astronauts to circle the lunar body entered a region of utter silence, totally cut off in a way no human has ever been. One astronaut described the barren expanse they encountered as a vast loneliness. Like spans of nothing, another said. Some cowboy had clipped the photograph from a magazine and stuck it on the wall.

On the counter nearby, I pick up a tally sheet from a poker game played years before. Tired from a day's work, three cowpunchers sat here cutting the cards beneath a photo of the moon. They played only a few hands before turning in, letting the trajectory of sleep carry them into a deeper night.

Milzer walks over to the photo. "It doesn't look too different," he says, "from where we are."

With snow falling outside, the two of us talk over what to do. I've known Milzer since grade school, so we don't need a lot of words to get our ideas across. One option is to fire up the stove and wait until the storm passes. But then we'll have to face the sand ridge in the morning when it might be buried under a foot of snow. We agree to keep moving, making a decision not much different from the one that got us stuck here in the first place.

Snow continues falling as we leave the line cabin on Paria Plateau and walk back to the pickup. Crossing the dirt track, we check the slope for another route and eliminate all but one possibility. The truck has to hit it at just the right angle to make it up. Once committed there won't be time for second thoughts.

Part of me wants to hold back, but there's little choice. We return to the truck, and Milzer climbs in the back to add weight over the rear wheels for more traction. I put it in gear and take off.

The truck shoots up the ridge, swerving between a fallen tree and a clump of yucca. It pitches and rolls like a rudderless boat, almost churning to a stop, almost losing momentum. Milzer braces himself to keep from ricocheting around the back. A band of sky quickly appears in the windshield as the slope levels. We're flying across the ridge before I realize we've topped out. Unable to stop and unable to slow down, I push on toward solid ground as the snow keeps falling.

Darkness rises through the cloud cover so slowly neither of us notices when full night arrives. A half-foot of snow has fallen by the time we reach the west flank of the Paria and descend into House Rock Valley. We intersect a dirt road slick with snow and follow it north, sliding on the steeper grades. Barely making it to the paved highway, I turn the truck into the storm, not sure where we will end up that night.

Wind blows the snow straight toward the windshield, reducing visibility to no farther than the front of the hood. Milzer looks glum. He came on this trip to spend some time in the dry desert before heading to Alaska. But shortly before he arrived, the weather turned. Winter switched places with spring, the way it does sometimes.

Some people travel for a change of weather, some to change the very pattern of their lives. For me, travel has become part of the pattern, a rhythm pulling me away from home and bringing me back to it. It has become part of the work I do. Sometimes I travel to find a story, but this time it's to find a way of telling one. I need a chance to ease into it, letting the miles draw the words out. For the moment, it's enough to let the motion of the trip stir the past, the way the rush of wind shakes the brush on the side of the road. It's enough to begin remembering.

Hidden by the storm, the distance ahead dissolves into a span of time endured, sinking into a deeper matrix. As I drive, thoughts drop back through the years, back to the day I first heard about this country.

Mad Kelly

A man leaned far over the railing, flapping his arms like he wanted to fly, looking straight at me.

"Come on up," he shouted from the terrace of the university's student union building in Tucson. He might have been drunk, crazy, or just born-again. Anything was possible. I kept walking, pretending not to hear.

"Don't be afraid," he said, singling me out. "Come on up, I have something to teach you." Only a few students straggled through the open arcade at this time of year. The desert heat kept most inside. I was on a mail run, having put aside my anthropology books only to fall into a situation stranger than the customs I'd been reading about. Giving in to curiosity, I climbed the steps and wondered what I was getting myself into.

The man wore a rumpled white shirt, with sleeves rolled to mid-forearm, and a tuft of beard growing from his chin. He appeared to have stepped from an old news clip of a 1950s Ban-the-Bomb march and had the intensity to match. He stared at me with dark eyes too tightly focused. "I hope you're not in a hurry," he said. "We have important work to do. I have a lesson in the calculus of people to give you."

As I took a seat, he continued. "My name is Kelly. Kelly stands for Celt. It's pronounced with a 'k' sound like the *Book of Kells*. I'm a Celtic magician," he added matter-of-factly.

Moving beyond the preliminaries, Kelly took a step closer and tilted his head. He seemed to be waiting for an answer to a question he hadn't asked. I sat there uncomfortably, not speaking. "You are a shepherd," he said, "although you may not know it."

My self-appointed teacher ran to his leather shoulder bag on a nearby table and began rummaging through it. "Where are my pipes?" he wondered, talking to himself. "I thought I left them here. Well, it doesn't matter." He spun around. "Here!"

Standing stiff-backed, Kelly placed his hands in front of his mouth, fingering an imaginary flute. He began to dance with high prancing steps, throwing his head back and forth while singing in a thin, archaic voice. After a few steps, he stopped next to me.

"The Great Pan is dead," he said with a smile and moved his face to within a few inches of mine, studying my expression with unblinking eyes. His stare was unsettling, crazy.

"Don't be afraid," he said. "I won't transgress the private areas of your mind." He spread out his arms on each side of my head and snapped his fingers without breaking his gaze. A second later he snapped them again before letting his arms drop.

"I'm a shepherd of wholeness," he said with deep sadness. "And so are you."

A light run of piano music came from a room across the terrace. Kelly cocked his head and listened. All at once he whirled around and ran toward the sound, disappearing into a far room. The music stopped short. Soon a batch of ominous notes, each pounded and warped with intensity, rolled off the keyboard. The music ended as quickly as it started, and the magician sprinted back with a wide smile. "I've played that piece on two other pianos in Tucson. I only need a fourth to complete the quadrant."

Before I could ask a question, he began intoning a list of Celtic kings and battles set to rhyme. I had trouble following the recitation, but he again stopped abruptly. "I am a good magician," he said, turning to the south and looking up at the sky, "but the moon is past full."

Tucson draws its share of saints and madmen. I asked Kelly what he was doing so far from home. Fall in the desert must have been hard on him, far from trees and the wind-driven leaves. He began pacing next to the railing.

"I am a professor of illogic engaged in the calculus of people. I am the gray man existing without good or evil." He kept silent for a moment as he walked back and forth. "I am just out of a mental institution where I spent over two years in yoga solitude. Some people call it therapy."

His pacing grew faster, more frantic. Kelly explained that before a judge committed him, he danced for the flower children on the streets of Boulder. But they only looked at him strangely. They had all been created together, he said, and couldn't understand a dance of loneliness.

At some point in his travels Kelly found his way to the Four Corners country, a place I had never seen. His face opened in wonder as he spoke about the only place where four states converged, forming a cross. He stood rigid with his arms stretched wide. "Four—the sacred number," he said, "the four worlds of the Indians, the fourth dimension. It's the spiritual heart of the continent."

Distracted by a stray thought, Kelly let his arms slump. But I reminded him about the calculus of people, and he leaped to his bag and pulled out a small metal drum. The magician began to dance in a stiff, goat-legged manner, keeping time with thumps on the drum. Turning toward me he began chanting in a full voice, "Bummmm-bummmm, the establishment."

Kelly stepped closer. "Bummm, the establishment. Bummm, the establishment. Bummmmmmmmm," he drew out the last note and abruptly cut it off. "BUM!" He hit the drum and shouted "THE TRAP DOOR!" with his eyes bulging like a man hanging from a gallows. For a couple of measures he stood rigid. Then singing in an eerie falsetto his voice dropped down the scale,

"Dee-
    dee-
       dee-
          dee."

He finished with just two words: "The Fool."

Putting the drum down, he smiled. "Well, it wasn't perfect," he said, "but it was right. That's your lesson. You must learn imperfection in the right way—the crack in the cup, the break in the pattern, the . . ."

He stopped in mid-sentence, listening to something I couldn't hear. "I have to go," he said, shouldering his bag, "but I'll be there when you need me."

"Where are you going?"

"To the record store to sing along with the piped-in music." He turned and flew down the stairs.

I never did run into Kelly again. But in the months ahead I thought about the Four Corners country he had described, intrigued by what might lie in that direction. Whether it was into a deeper myth or only the other side of somewhere else, I had yet to discover.

Sun Chief

That winter I left Tucson with Scott Milzer, driving north on my first trip into the high desert of the Four Corners. In a few days, my friend had to report for duty. He was on his way to Vietnam.

Earlier, Milzer had written me a cryptic letter from college. In it he described a flash of enlightenment he had experienced in his backyard. It came like a sudden rift in the clouds. His studies seemed beside the point after that, so he stopped attending classes. This gave the draft board their chance, and they quickly selected him to serve his senior year in Vietnam. When I asked for more details about what happened in his backyard, he only shrugged. "I guess," he said, "those things come and go."

Sunlight ignited a line of faraway cliffs as the highway crossed high above the Little Colorado River. We entered the Painted Desert, moving quickly over the surface of things through the deep light of late afternoon. The two of us were on our way to the Hopi mesas to look for Don Talayesva, a Sun Clan leader. The road stretched ahead without a curve, spanning the distance as if suspended in air.

A reservation dog trotted along the roadside with its nose close to the ground, scavenging on the run. Another sat by a deserted bead stand, waiting for a reason to move. Behind it, a thin column of smoke gave away the location of a mud-roofed hogan, planted among the badland hills.

"I heard," Milzer said, "that the Navajos have two ways of looking at the landscape. One's with hard eyes and the other's with soft eyes. Hard eyes are used when looking for things like game, water, pop machines. Soft eyes are used to take in the beauty of the scene." He looked out the window at hummocks of rock stripped to bare colors of weathered blue and purple.

Shadows trickled down the folds of the escarpment flanking the highway. The road veered toward it, swinging left and right, hunting the best route up. Under the slanting light, the cliffs emitted a red thick with layered hues.

Approaching Tuba City, we passed a barren cornfield with a scarecrow planted at one end. A Navajo farmer had nailed a headless raven onto a post with its wings spread wide as a warning to other birds. A cluster of hogans gave way to low-bid government housing as we entered Tuba. Mormon settlers named the town after Tuvi, a Hopi outcast living here when they first arrived. A sign in front of a store advertised "Hamburgers, Burritos, Hen Scratch."

Stopping for a cup of coffee, I briefed Milzer on what I had learned about Talayesva from an anthropology professor. The Hopi leader had been raised in a traditional home until the age of seven when the Indian Agency forced him to leave his village and attend boarding school. They cut his hair and taught him Christian prayers and how to salute the flag. When he turned twelve, the school authorities let him choose between staying in California and returning to his old way of life. He chose to go home and live the life of a traditional Hopi.

At fifty he wrote his autobiography, *Sun Chief,* a book still studied in college classes. Now eighty, Talayesva had lived another thirty years. "That's another book," I said, "another book he never wrote."

Turning toward the Hopi mesas, our road climbed a plateau bordering Moenkopi Wash. The Red Cloud, a borrowed VW bug, was losing power on the grade, barely making the hill. As the car slowed to a crawl, Milzer jumped out to lighten the load. He ran alongside, wearing a tweed jacket and Navy watch cap.

As the road leveled, Milzer hopped in. We crossed the plateau and followed the rim of Third Mesa to the Hopi village of Old Oraibi, the home of the Sun Chief. Nestled together, the stone houses appeared as old as the rock that fell away in fractured cliffs below them. Leaving the car, we walked down a dirt track pressed between flat-roofed houses, stacked in tiers two and three stories high. Patches of stucco had crumbled from some walls and none stood square. The angles, slightly skewed, gave the houses a hand-molded appearance. We walked through the old pueblo, held by the last traces of light in the west.

A path forked to the ruins of a church, standing exposed on the tip of the mesa. Missionaries had built it near a Hopi shrine over the protest of traditional leaders. The missionaries eventually abandoned it after lightning struck repeatedly, finally catching the structure on fire. Someone had carved on the threshold an enigmatic message reading, "We were not here."

Wandering back through Old Oraibi, I felt disoriented. On foot in one of the oldest inhabited villages in America, I found all the familiar patterns had shifted. Nothing made sense.

We returned to the plaza looking for someone to give us directions to Talayesva's house. No one was about. Walking down a back lane, I noticed a faint light leaking from a window curtained with sackcloth. We kept walking, having second thoughts about the whole trip. But we had come too far; I had to make an attempt.

Turning back to the house with a light, I knocked on the door. A voice within called out in a language I didn't understand. Hesitating a moment, I opened the door.

The interior walls stood bare, washed in the dull yellow of a kerosene lantern turned low. They enclosed a man and woman, born in another century, who sat by a metal table in the corner. The room held nothing else.

"We're looking for Don Talayesva," I said. "Do you know where he lives?"

The old man looked at us, in no hurry to answer. He wore his hair cut square in front and knotted in back. Finally he spoke in a surprisingly strong voice. "He is waiting for you down below."

"Down below?"

"Yes, down there. He is waiting for you."

We thanked him and left, more confused than before. I hadn't notified anyone we were coming. Talayesva had no idea we were here to see him.

"That was spooky," Milzer said once we were outside. "No way I'm going any further."

"What did he mean by 'down there'?" I wondered.

"Who knows? He's probably talking about the underworld. This is far enough. Let's get out of here."

The two of us turned back, retracing our steps to the car. We walked through a night broken only by a single light shining far out on the desert below the mesa. Driving beyond the village, we found a protruding ledge to throw our sleeping bags beneath. Rain started to fall, soft and gentle.

Falling asleep, I began to dream. Frightened by something in the dream, I tried to wake up but couldn't. I was aware of being trapped in the dream, conscious but still asleep. For what must have been an hour, I struggled to wake up. Growing exhausted, I finally gave up, and as soon as I stopped trying, I awoke.

Milzer was already sitting up, staring into the dark beyond the mouth of the overhang. A gust of wind shook the brush. "Did you see it?" he asked.

"See what?"

"A kachina. Right out there."

At first light we gathered our gear and left. My meeting with Talayesva would have to wait. I needed some distance to make sense of this place and to sort out the unfamiliar layering of past and present.

Back in Tucson I picked up *Sun Chief* again and read Tala-yesva's story of the Salt Journey. With two other Hopi Indians he entered the Grand Canyon in 1912, leaving prayer feathers at shrines as they descended. He was undertaking a journey, part pilgrimage and part rite of passage, to gather salt along the Colorado River. With faces painted red, the Hopi traveled into a region where the line separating the living and the dead was no longer clearly drawn.

Talayesva's account of the trip conveyed a sense of the world so different from my own I became curious. A year later, using his book as a guide, I decided to retrace the route with Milzer and my brother John. Both of them had returned from Vietnam after completing tours of duty in different regions of the country. Both were ready for a long hike; where they ended up didn't matter. Walking the Hopi Salt Trail was the first trip the three of us would make together. I don't remember the last.

Before leaving, I asked a Hopi if it was okay to use the trail. "Yes," he said hesitantly and turned to leave. "But if you go," he added, "you go at your own risk."

On the rim of the Little Colorado Gorge we found a weathered rock marking the trailhead. This was where Talayesva said a Hopi spirit, the younger War Twin, had turned himself into stone so others could find their way. The three of us began to descend, wearing layers of wool and down against the cold and carrying odds and ends of gear picked up at surplus stores.

Below the trail marker, a vague route dropped through a natural break in the cliffs. We worked our way beneath the rimrock and zigzagged into the gorge, surrounded by unfamiliar terrain. We could match only a few landmarks to the crowded contour lines on the map. The pattern of the canyons had not yet shifted into focus for us. It was all new, unsorted. We were heading for the junction of two rivers, somewhere deep in a tangle of cliffs.

Our route led above sheer drops with unsure footing, past shrines we didn't recognize, and down to the Little Colorado. The river threaded along as pale blue as a strand of turquoise. We turned downstream, bushwhacking through tamarisk thickets, not realizing we were taking the hard way.

Pushing along the riverbank for a couple of hours brought us to a place so unusual we immediately recognized it from the written description. A travertine dome, thirty feet long and twenty high, curved above the river. White minerals streaked down the sides of the flat-topped, earth-red mound. For the Hopi, this was the original kiva holding the *sipapu,* both the place of emergence and the direct entrance to an underworld inhabited by the spirits of the dead. The atmosphere was solemn, mythic.

"Is it okay to go up?" John asked. We hesitated, unsure if we should climb it, wondering how to act in a place others held sacred. Not knowing, we fell back on Talayesva's account. We took off our boots and walked barefoot up the north side as he had done.

A ragged hole on top dropped a few feet to a pool of sulfurous-green water. Prayer feathers hung below the rim marking the four directions. These ritual offerings came as a surprise. I was told the Hopi no longer made the salt trek, since only men too old to negotiate the trail knew the route. But someone had been here within the past year.

As we stood at the opening, the waters below began to move. A line of bubbles broke the surface. For the Hopi, the spring formed a thin boundary between worlds. At this place the ancestors of all people had left the underworld and climbed through the opening. They reached the earth's surface where we now live, the fourth and last world. Europeans had found their New World by staying on the surface of things and pushing farther west. The Hopi found theirs by a long ascent, climbing into the next configuration.

After emerging, each people headed a different direction on the path given them. The Hopi further separated as individual clans left to find the center of all things. Their search became a spiritual migration toward a place whose name they did not know. On their travels they looked for signs, letting the destination reveal itself. Eventually they were drawn to the stark mesas where the clans gathered together again, the mesas where the Hopi now live. Each time the clouds rise up and drift across the desert bringing rain, the emergence is renewed.

Continuing down the canyon, we walked through an immense natural ruin. What hadn't collapsed appeared to balance on the verge of collapse. We passed beneath high cliffs, heaved upward by the slow push of time until exposed by erosion. They stood thousands of feet above the floor of the canyon, hanging for a geologic moment, waiting to be taken by the pull of gravity. We walked through the stillness of that moment and reached the confluence late in the day. With boots slung around our necks, we stepped into the Little Colorado.

"Ay, Chi-hua-hua!" John shouted. The sudden cold of the water numbed the legs to a dull ache as we waded across, waist-deep. On the far side of the river we started a warming fire with the tinder we had stuffed in our boots. The three of us huddled around the flames to dry off as the blue waters of the river emptied into the green Colorado.

The current of the great river pulled deeper into the cut below us, the gateway to the Grand Canyon. When Talayesva and his companions reached the Colorado they placed prayer feathers on the water for the waves to carry away. Not knowing the prayers, I let it take my thoughts with it.

After cooking our food we talked some, avoiding anything that touched on the past or the future. No one mentioned the war; our plans for the future were vague. The conversation tapered off as we watched the cliffs of Cape Solitude grow red in the withdrawing light. "That's an unusual color," Milzer said, "kind of a Burnt Norton."

When the Hopi camped here after gathering salt downriver, the war chief warned young Talayesva not to look at the rock walls. Throughout the expedition, the older man had kept his curiosity in check. Knowledge, the Hopi believe, should come through initiation. Inappropriate knowledge can be dangerous. The leader told Talayesva a story about an earlier expedition when a man saw the face of a girl in the canyon walls and returned to his village to find his sister had died. Stare at a cliff face long enough and the human face begins to emerge.

Across the Colorado, sunlight glinted off bits of metal scattered on the side of a butte, artifacts of the world we had left behind. Years before, two passenger jets crashed at the confluence after a midair collision. A Hopi once told me about a prophesy he had heard as a young boy before the invention of airplanes. An old man told him that one day people would travel on roads up in the air. The boy wondered how that could be. "Then one day it happened," he said. "It's there, today. People up there, flying around like birds."

My brother studied the wreckage and tried to plot the flight paths of the aircraft. He had piloted helicopters in Vietnam but stopped flying when he left the army, finding it too entangled with a way of thinking he wanted to leave behind. "There's no pattern to it," he finally said, letting the problem rest.

Light withdrew to the highest rim of cliffs and then higher. No one spoke. It was a moment suspended, pulled between two forces, one geologic and the other mythic. One was timeless and the other so weighted with time as to be much the same thing.

Lying in the dark, I listened to the river sweep around the bend, running deep, and then deeper.

Night at the foot of Third Mesa. I stood on the roof of a kiva with a friend, Carolyn Brown, a couple of years after my first trip to find the Sun Clan leader. Long ends of a ladder pushed through the smokehole of the ceremonial chamber, reaching into the nightsky. It was midwinter, Powamuya, the month of the cleansing moon. Somewhere on the mesa above stood Old Oraibi, unseen in the dark.

Hollow drumming came from far away, felt more than heard as it resonated through the village of Kykotsmovi. A line of kachinas filed around the corner of a house, startling a dog that scooted away with its tail tucked low. The ancestral spirits called to each other in voices shaped like the wind, "Woo, woo, woooo."

A Hopi keeping watch at the kiva entryway invited us inside. I hadn't expected this, having read somewhere that kivas were closed to outsiders and women. Climbing down the ladder, I found Hopi women and children packed into the back of the room. Visitors from other villages crowded together on a bench running along the wall. A lantern tied to the center beam gave light. Prayer feathers dangled from the rafters in one corner. Taking a seat on the bench, we waited.

This trip to the Hopi mesas had happened impulsively. That afternoon in Flagstaff, I'd mentioned to Carolyn my earlier attempt to talk with the Sun Chief. "I know Don," she told me. "He's a friend of mine. You need to meet him."

Within a couple of hours we were on our way to the Hopi mesas, arriving late Saturday evening during a Night Dance.

A shout came from outside the kiva. The kachinas had arrived. The fire keeper, standing below the smokehole, called out a welcome to the spirits of his people. Kachinas began climbing down the ladder, one by one. Arcane symbols painted with red ocher, yellow, and black covered their bare chests. Cotton sashes held in place the kilts embroidered in green, red, and black designs. Bristling with feathers, the Hopi spirits pressed into the chamber, milling about and calling to each other in a strange tongue.

A low drumming began, sounding like the rumble of distant thunder. Order emerged as the kachinas formed their dance line, curving around the kiva with one side left open. I sat straight-backed, trying to make more room as the kachinas pressed close. A priest passed down the line of dancers, sprinkling each with sacred corn, ground dust-fine.

The solid bench reverberated with the heavy boom of a drum, again and again, as the air within the chamber moved in pulses. It felt as if I were hearing my own heartbeat for the first time. At the same instant, the lead kachina shook his rattle so loudly the hairs prickled on the back of my neck.

Kachinas began to dance and chant in unison, marking time with turtle shell rattles tied to their legs. The line of dancers moved forward a step or two, reversed direction, and returned to the starting point. The dance turned back on itself, again and again, as steady as the turn of the seasons. I found myself pulled within the colors and sounds.

At times it was all too close, too intense. I averted my eyes, looking instead at the moccasined feet or the shadows moving rhythmically across the wall. I watched a little girl, sitting on her grandmother's lap, as the shadows of the kachinas played across her open face. For a hundred years observers had predicted the dying out of these ceremonies. The fascination in her eyes told a different story.

Next morning, Carolyn and I drove to Talayesva's house in Old Oraibi. His daughter invited us inside to wait for his return. Sunlight warmed the wall of a room, sparsely furnished but not empty. The women cooked as the children dodged about, and older voices drifted from a backroom. "He will soon be home from church," she told us.

This came as a surprise. It meant that the *tawa mongwi*, the Sun Clan leader who had rejected the outside world to follow the life of a traditional Hopi, had become a Christian. The daughter also mentioned that his grandson was being initiated into one of the ceremonial societies that weekend. Talayesva's conversion, she said, had caused some uneasiness in the home. And I was certain our presence, politely tolerated, only added to the awkwardness of the situation.

An hour later the old Hopi appeared, bending low through a

sidedoor. He wore his gray hair cut short in a style brought back to the mesas by returning veterans. After shaking hands, he invited us to share a meal of traditional foods prepared for his grandson's ceremony. Curious, I took a bite of unfamiliar bread, shaped in a lump as pale yellow as dust.

As we ate, the Sun Chief spoke. "I am very old," he told us. "I will not live long. I have lost my hearing. My memory will soon follow."

After eating in silence for a while, the Hopi put aside his food. He began to talk about losing his wife two years before. Her death came as a tremendous blow to him. "I was sad all the time," he said. "Everyday I go into my fields and cry. I can't work. I go back home and go to sleep and dream. Each night this terrible angel comes to warn me."

The old man paused, reluctant to continue.

"What did the angel tell you?" asked Carolyn.

"Each night I see the same angel," he said. "It tells me I will spend eternity in hell unless I become a Christian." Frightened, Talayesva asked a missionary for advice. To end the dreams, he was told, he must give up his traditional ways.

Before I could ask any questions, Talayesva began telling us about the time he talked to a group of college students. "They asked childish questions," he said. "Nobody talked about what was important."

As he continued talking, I listened, keeping my questions to myself. What I had to ask was no longer necessary. Wanting to make sense out of my life, I came to these mesas looking for something tangible, a fixed point to get my bearings. I wanted to find a place called Old Oraibi, embedded in its thousand years.

But instead of a cultural artifact I found a living community where a man was struggling with his own identity. I expected to hear the voice of an old Hopi praying for rain, but instead found a man running from angels. Meeting Talayesva, I realized we can only live the way of life we're given. No other.

Saying goodbye, the two of us stepped outside. A yellow dog lay curled in the shade beneath an empty basketball hoop. We crossed the plaza where the kachinas dance and left Third Mesa.

The Singer

An old man in a cowboy hat walked past a hogan, chanting to himself in a rolling monotone. Jim Sampson was a Navajo singer, a medicine man.

My brother and I followed him to the sheep corral. He stopped and spoke a few words, formed deep in his throat, drawn out and chopped short. He didn't speak English; John and I didn't speak Navajo.

The singer looked at us with a smile that deepened the creases in his face. Facing out, he swept his arm toward a wide expanse of sand and rock. He wore a leather bowguard, set with cast silver, on his left wrist. Forming the shape of the sun with his thumb and forefinger, he swung his arm in an arc above his head, stopping at the meridian. He then reached out with both arms and drew them back to his chest. I took this to mean he wanted us to herd the sheep in that direction and bring them back at noon. Jim Sampson walked off with a smile, singing to himself.

Looking in the direction he had indicated, I didn't see anything out there a sheep might want to eat. Prickly brush topped sand hummocks that supported a few tufts of grass. John opened the corral gate. As sheep and goats bunched their way through the opening, we began our first morning as sheepherders.

For some time the Navajo sheepman had realized he was getting too old to take care of his herd during the winter. But he didn't want to sell them and go on welfare. His identity was tied closely to his herd. He liked having them around. Since the younger relatives either worked or attended school, he had come up with another idea.

Jim and his wife Alice had offered us room and board to take care of the sheep, but no pay. We would eat meals with them and sleep in our own hogan. The arrangement gave me an opportunity to get close to this region and its people. My brother had his own reasons for being here. They had something to do with Vietnam. He was looking for empty skies and long, open days.

A ragged line of sheep and goats filed out of the Navajo camp. John brought up the rear, wearing fatigue pants and a Montagnard bracelet. He had stopped shaving the day he left the army and now wore a full beard. I kept near the front, dressed in jeans and an old mountain parka to cut the wind. We knew little about the Navajo people and less about sheep.

The morning passed chasing strays, trying to keep together the herd of about a hundred head. We had to stay alert to prevent stragglers from falling behind and to turn the leaders when they drifted too far in one direction. The Angora goats, with long fleecy coats, took the lead. The sheep followed, content to be carried along by the flock. The animals flowed across the land in pulses, nibbling dry stalks of grass, running, nibbling again. They moved in a living mat, white against the yellow cast of the sand.

Returning at noon, already tired, we caught the aroma of piñon smoke from the cookstove. We guided the sheep through the homestead, passing two hogans and a four-sided house known as a *kin,* a shed, a horse corral, and a car hulk used as a chicken coop. Some traditionals shift between a winter camp and a summer camp to follow the grass and milder weather, but Jim and Alice had settled into one place.

They owned very little but were not burdened by a sense of poverty. Alice only had the right to graze sheep and have a hogan on a certain piece of land owned by the Navajo tribe. They once explained it by saying the land didn't belong to them, they belonged to the land. Their real wealth lay in the life they invested in the people around them. They had few possessions but were at home where they lived.

We penned the sheep in the corral, a circle of ax-cut juniper poles slanting inward, and broke for lunch. After eating, Jim led us outside and gestured in the opposite direction from the one we took that morning. Two camp dogs came with us this time, trotting at the fringes of the herd. I don't think they had names. One of them was called "the dog with the black tail," but only to tell it apart from the one without distinguishing marks. Not trained as sheep dogs, their job was to guard against coyotes and to warn us when strangers approached. I never saw them do either.

That evening John and I dragged ourselves back to our hogan, an octagon of peeled logs notched together at each corner. A stovepipe poked through a smokehole cut through the peak of the roof. The door faced east to catch the first light from the rising sun.

Stretched out on a goat skin next to the potbelly stove, I watched Orion cross the nightsky far above the smokehole. As I began drifting off to sleep, Joe Daisy, one of the English-speaking relatives, came by to talk. Every morning, he said, we had to take the herd to water at the trading post four miles away. There was nothing for them to drink here. It hadn't rained for a long time. Tomorrow, Jim Sampson would show us the trail to the Tonalea Trading Post at Red Lake.

At dawn I woke to someone pounding on the door. One of the grandchildren had been sent to get us moving. A boy, about seven years old, entered. We later learned he lived with his parents nearby but often stayed with Jim and Alice. "Eat!" he shouted. "My grandmother says 'Eat!'"

John and I pulled on our boots and shambled down to the main house. A partition wall divided it into two rooms with sleeping quarters in the back and a combination kitchen, weaving studio, and livestock nursery in the front. As we sat down at a metal table to eat, Alice grabbed a lamb from a cardboard box next to the stove and began to feed it with a bottle.

Her hair was pulled back, showing silver earrings. She wore a velveteen overshirt and a full skirt cut from wine-colored satin and gathered at the waist. She was a strong woman with a physical presence more imposing than her husband's. The day before, I spotted her chopping firewood, swinging a double-bladed ax with ease. Alice was the matriarch, the center of a large, extended family.

She had cooked a full breakfast for us. A stack of thick tortilla-style fry bread sat next to two enamel bowls of cornmeal mush with fried eggs on the side. The table held even more food than yesterday. We had been told it was the custom to eat everything placed before us. The woman would be offended if we didn't eat what she served. So we dutifully set to work on breakfast, barely managing to finish.

Outside, we joined Jim Sampson at the horse corral. The Navajo chanter, as lean as a juniper pole, had been out saying a prayer to the dawn. He led his saddled horse to the sheep pen and mounted as we opened the gate. Again he sang a low chant as the goats and sheep left the corral.

The three of us crossed the sweep of high desert at an un-hurried pace. The horseman trailed the herd, moving without wasted effort. Anticipating every move of the sheep, he was right where he needed to be at each moment. He never raised his voice and never got angry at the animals. This was the first lesson he gave us in herding sheep, and the last.

A conical butte, called "The Peak Where Wildcats Stretch," broke the horizon. Closer to us, a massive outcrop of sandstone humped above the flats, and a wind-rippled dune slid down the side of a wash. Stiff clumps of narrow-leaf yucca and snakeweed anchored the sandy ridges. Riding through the dry beauty of the land, the old man kept singing to himself.

As we neared the trading post, the herd poured over the mesa rim and headed straight for the shrunken pools at Red Lake. We took turns watching the sheep and visiting the trading post. It sat on a rise above the water, built with multiple sides in an at-tempt to resemble a hogan. The stone building served as post office, grocery and feed store, a pawn shop, and gas station. A half-dozen pickup trucks were parked in front. An older Navajo stood by the door, wearing a single turquoise earring and a hair knot wrapped with cotton cord. He exchanged the day's news with a young man in an Arizona Feeds cap.

Leaving the desert glare, I stepped into the dark interior and heard the Anglo trader speaking Navajo to a customer. Cases of soda pop and bags of flour were stacked in front of a high counter. Most of the items for sale were shelved behind it. The store sold canned goods and enamel cookware, tack and Pendleton blankets, snack foods. The trader stayed busy dealing with customers or rearranging his stock. A young Navajo woman worked behind the counter, wearing traditional jewelry but with her hair styled for town. I introduced myself and mentioned we would be getting our mail here for the winter.

"We already know about you," she said. "Is it true you are herding their sheep?" The idea of having *bilagaanas,* white men, herd her family's sheep intrigued her. "Where can we get a couple of sheepherders?"

Within a few days, John and I had eased into a routine. Each morning we woke up to what had become a daily ritual—"Eat! My grandmother says 'Eat!' "

By now we dreaded the thought of facing another breakfast. The old woman kept serving us more food each morning. Glumly walking to Alice's house, we sat down at the table before six pieces of thick fry bread, a can of butter, a bowl of mush, a dozen eggs, and a pot of coffee.

Enough. We wanted to accommodate their customs, but we just couldn't eat any more. Taking only what food we needed, we left the rest untouched. As we walked to the corral, we wondered if this breach of etiquette might jeopardize our relationship with the family.

That night Joe, who had fallen into the role of mediator, stopped by the hogan. He looked puzzled when we apologized for not finishing breakfast. Suddenly he began to laugh, realizing what had been happening. "No," he said. "Don't feel bad."

His wife, he told us, had warned Alice that bilagaanas had big appetites so she better give us plenty to eat. The first morning Alice had served what she thought were generous portions. When we ate everything, she was afraid she wasn't feeding us enough. So she gave us more the next morning, and more the next, wondering where we put all the food.

Joe politely mentioned another mix-up. We had learned the Navajo word for "thank you," and used it liberally. Accustomed to thanking someone for normal courtesies, we did the same with Jim and Alice. Traditionally, a Navajo reserves thanks for unexpected and out-of-the-ordinary assistance. To thank someone for a small favor sends a message that being polite is not their normal way of acting. It implies they haven't been raised properly.

After Joe's talk, we rationed our thanks like proper Navajos. But by then the old couple had learned our custom, and for the rest of our stay passed out thanks like Anglos. The Navajo family began to realize we knew a lot less than they first thought.

At the end of the first week, my brother and I were returning from the trading post when one of the ewes flopped down and refused to move. She bleated as the flock drifted away, worried the other sheep were leaving her behind. Sheep have a powerful urge to herd.

We first thought the ewe was sick. But a moment later it became obvious why she was lying on the trail. A newborn lamb struggled into the light of day, the sand clinging to its wet nose. No one had warned us about this possibility, taking it for granted we could recognize a pregnant sheep. Although John had delivered human babies when he worked with a rescue squad as a teenager, sheep were different. The new mother nervously looked at the departing herd, barely noticing her lamb.

After giving it a lick or two, the ewe climbed onto her legs, growing more frantic. She took a few steps toward the herd and a few steps back to the lamb, split between two urges. But the desire to be with the herd won out and she trotted after the other sheep. Wet and shivering, the abandoned lamb stood on wobbly legs. I picked it up in my arms, not knowing what else to do, and held it close to my body for warmth. John got the herd turned, and we walked back to the home camp.

Alice stood by the corral, waiting for us to come up the trail. When she saw me carrying the newborn lamb, she gave a cry that turned into a laugh. She grabbed the lamb from me by the front legs and carried it into the house. Alice now had another lamb to bottle feed. Joe showed up again that night with instructions on how to handle the animals during lambing. Once a mother rejects her young, he told us, she won't take it back.

Either by design or default, winter was lambing season for the herd. Among the older Navajo, winter was also the time for storytelling. The old men save their stories for the long nights that come after the first frost of autumn and before the first strike of lightning in the spring.

One evening we joined Jim and Alice in the main house where many of the relatives had gathered. The old woman had butchered a sheep that day. I watched her take the severed head and singe off the wool in a small fire of woodchips. She carried the blackened lump into the house, the eyes two glowing embers and the smell of burnt wool hanging in the air.

After we ate mutton stew, Jim Sampson told a story about the creation of the world. His version differed from others I had read.

"Long-time-ago," he began, drawing his listeners back with him as he drew out the phrase, "the earth was as small as a fist."

The old man clenched his hand before him and continued. "The earth started growing by adding knowledge. With each new thought it grew larger and larger. When all thoughts had ended and all knowledge was accumulated, the earth stopped growing.

"During this time the Holy People were in need of moisture. They grew a yucca plant and made lots of suds from the roots. With these they blew out a path to each direction. Today these are seen as the clouds which bring rain."

The light of a lantern glinted in the eyes of the old man as he fleshed out his story, adding details and repeating key phrases. "At that time," he continued, "men existed in the world below in the form of animals. There was no sun, only dawn. And people did not call each other by name. Only one of them, a man with two flutes, knew the secret of reaching this world. But he couldn't tell the others until they discovered his name. Once they found the right name to call him, his spirit grew like a seed into a hollow reed. Through this plant the people climbed into this world.

"In the next world, close upon us," he said, "we will return to the beginning, to what we were then. We will pull on the bird skins and furs in a place where no one wants to call another by name."

The sky passed through the gray-blue shift of dawn. Dishwater, thrown from the hogan, flashed in the first wave of light over the east rise. The winds picked up, increasing in force as the day grew.

Tired after a couple of hours of facing into the weather, my brother and I took shelter in a calm pocket behind a ridge. John removed his can of Prince Albert and rolled a cigarette. As we sat overlooking the treeless expanse, he began talking about flying in the jungles of Vietnam.

He rarely talked about the war. What I knew had come in episodes separated by long weeks when he said nothing, episodes strewn with names like Dak To, Hill 875, Tet. He talked with bitterness about the waste of lives but missed that intensity of living. And he talked with passion about the flying he had walked away from.

Looking into these vacant spaces, John remembered a mission where he was surrounded by green. A patrol had fallen into an ambush, he said, and radioed for a pullout from a landing zone deep in the jungle. Finding a hole in the canopy just wide enough for his chopper, he dropped deep into the green well of vegetation. The rotor blades circled only inches from the trees, clipping a leaf now and again.

He had to fly by thought alone. Holding the controls without moving his hands, he only had to think where he wanted to go and the helicopter followed. The chopper eased through the trees to the landing zone where the survivors jumped onboard. His door gunner opened fire as they lifted up through the tunnel of green. With gunfire flashing from below, he kept his eye on the patch of blue above until reaching the open sky. Flying in the jungle taught him that danger comes from below.

John paused, looking across the slickrock barrens. The sheep hadn't drifted too far. The wind was keeping them tucked behind the ridge. "The desert's different," he said.

As we walked over this country, we found traces of an earlier people. Where a footpath dropped over the mesa, the prehistoric Anasazi had carved a group of petroglyphs on a cliff wall. An immense bighorn dominated the panel, its horns curving back like those of the goats we herded.

The glyph may have given the Navajo sheepmen an idea. They had used the alcove for the backwall of a corral, saving themselves from having to cut so many fence posts. The *chindi* fear is supposed to keep people away from Anasazi sites. Some call it a fear of ghosts, but it's more a fear of being exposed to a breakdown in the natural order, especially when someone dies before their time has come. The lingering chindi presence can enter the lives of those nearby, causing sickness and death. But the Navajo are a pragmatic people and sometimes will take the risk, especially if they only have half the fence posts needed for a corral.

One morning I was taking the herd along a rough bench, looking for grass. Passing a sandy pocket, I noticed the wind had uncovered a scatter of potsherds. A single rock rested on the surface among them. Looking closer, I saw beneath it the smooth ceramic curve of pottery. I lifted up the rock and found a Kayenta Anasazi bowl, unbroken. A bold geometric design covered the inner surface, black against white. Someone, centuries before, had hidden the bowl beneath the rock. I replaced it and took off after the sheep.

Over the next week, John and I discussed what to do with the find. Of all the options, only one made sense in the end. We returned to the site and covered the bowl with sand, leaving the artifact where I had found it.

Letting it remain in place gave us more satisfaction than having it gather dust on a shelf or sit warehoused in the back room of a museum. But leaving it had its risks. If it surfaced again someone might take it, an animal might step on it, moisture might seep into a hairline crack and freeze. But knowing the bowl remained where some Anasazi left it eight centuries ago was worth the chance.

Every few days, I heated water on the woodstove to shave; every three weeks we drove into town for a shower. Between trips, we washed our hair using pounded yucca roots. Each morning we took the herd to water, each afternoon to graze. Time came in two slices, light and dark. At night I fell asleep as slowly as the darkness rose in the east. In the morning, I woke up to a wide dawn growing above the horizon. Sometimes a sheepherder becomes isolated from the flow of words. Left to my own thoughts, I watched memories surface and heard the voices of people I hadn't thought about for years.

Alone with the herd one day, I heard an angry shout and turned. An old Navajo, dressed in black, was riding up at a gallop. He reined in his horse a few feet from me. I didn't know him. Wearing dark sunglasses and a black hat, he shouted orders in Navajo that I couldn't understand. The horse churned around in a circle as the rider pulled its head tightly to the side. Growing angrier at my lack of response, the stranger spurred off at a run.

Later I learned our presence in the community had led to a full-blown argument at the chapter house. The trouble had come from a family carrying on a feud with Alice's people. Anglo sheepherders were another item of contention in a long history of conflict between the families. At the chapter meeting, Alice forcefully came to our defense, convincing the community to support the decision of her family.

Bringing us onto the reservation had been a difficult decision for them. Most whites living on Navajo lands had arrived under the auspices of a church, university, or government. To invite outsiders into the community on their own initiative, the family had to accept full responsibility for our actions.

Before reaching their decision, the extended family had met twice prior to our arrival and again on our first night. We sat among them as each spoke in turn. They questioned us closely, asking about our parents and wondering why we lived so far from our family. The formal decision was left to Jim Sampson. But Alice spoke before him, and her words carried enough weight to swing the decision either way. "Yes," she said in Navajo, and Jim agreed.

We became adjunct members of a family whose differences reflected those within the wider Red Lake community. Joe and his wife were Christians, others belonged to the Native American Church, and some followed traditional Navajo practices. But these lines often blurred. Jim, the medicine man, prayed to Jesus at times; a relative who followed the peyote way of the Native American Church had a traditional ceremony sung over him. Being pragmatic people, they sampled the various offerings and took what worked from each.

Local politics tended to divide along the lines of family and religion. During the tribal elections, an argument broke out at the chapter house between the supporters for two of the three candidates for tribal chairman. Jim traded heated words with another old man. Fists flew, and the room erupted into a brawl as almost everyone was related to one man or the other. They restored order only after both sides agreed to erase the two controversial candidates from the slate. The Navajo voters were left with one remaining name, the candidate no one wanted.

One evening Joe Daisy asked if I could drive the old couple to another trading post the next day. Jim and Alice didn't own a car. If they needed to go somewhere, they went by horse. But a trip by horse to the distant trading post would take two days. Alice wanted to sell a rug and thought the local trader might not give her a fair price.

Over the winter, she had been weaving the rug on her upright loom. With the help of the other women she had carded the raw wool and handspun it into yarn. I had watched her boil the plants she had gathered for dye in an iron kettle. And I had seen her sit before her loom at night, weaving by the dim light of a lantern.

Her finished rug was the size of a double saddle blanket, about a yard wide and maybe two yards long. She had woven a Storm Pattern design with lightning connecting the winds in each corner and a storm house placed at the center. The elements of the pattern balanced in a dynamic way, bringing harmony to the design.

Finishing breakfast the next morning, John and I left to warm up the Volkswagen. The night had been cold, and the engine wouldn't turn over. After a few tries, John thought it must be a frozen fuel line and crawled underneath to see what he could do.

An hour later the car still wouldn't start. At that point Jim walked up, dressed in a high-crowned, stiff-brimmed hat and a turquoise necklace of many strands. Reading the situation at a glance, he began to chant.

Passing slowly around the car, the Navajo completed the circuit and waited by the front door. John reconnected the fuel line as I jumped in the front seat to try it again. The engine started right up, and the old singer climbed in with a smile on his face.

Alice heard the engine running and came out carrying her rug, rolled and tied. At the trading post, we waited in the car as she took the rug inside to negotiate a price. It wasn't long before she returned, smiling. I asked if she had gotten a good price. "Yes," she said in Navajo and held up three $10 bills and a few ones.

As spring approached, John was ready to travel. He wanted to continue his studies in Mexico. A winter in the desert had taken the edge off his anger and given him a nickname. The Navajo at the trading post now called him Many Whiskers. I planned to stay a few extra weeks to help through the lambing season. We had met good people here, but it was time to move on. On my brother's last night, the relatives joked about finding us wives and invited us to stay forever.

After John left, the days grew longer. My nose burned and peeled for the first time all winter as the sunlight strengthened. With the change of seasons, the winds blew steadily. Sand thickened the air, drifting into the hogan and texturing the food. The lambing had tapered off, but the sheep began to scatter in search of the green shoots pushing up through the sand. It became harder to keep the herd together.

One morning, sunlight formed a faint ring as it scattered through a high cloud cover. Shards of prismatic light, called sun dogs, curved on each side of the halo. When I showed them to the old man, he reached into his pocket and pulled out a quartz crystal. He glanced through the clear stone and quickly put it away. As I continued to repair the corral, the medicine man saddled his horse and rode off.

Stormclouds gathered late in the day. Dark strands of rain swept down from the sky toward the parched ground. It hadn't rained all winter. The air held still and the land waited. I watched the dry rain brush so close I wanted to reach up and pull it down. But the moisture evaporated quicker than it fell. The rain never touched the earth.

Minutes later, a black ewe labored well and gave birth to twin lambs, one black and the other white. I rubbed the mother's milk on their noses to help them identify her. Picking up the lambs by the forelegs, I held them away from my body to keep my scent off them and make it easier for the mother to recognize their shapes.

At that moment, Jim came riding in from the distance. He carried a bundle of freshly dug roots thrown over the pommel. The old man smiled as I raised the lambs higher. He took them and draped both over the horse in front of him. *"Ya'at'eeh,"* he laughed and headed for home. "It is good."

That night Jim heard I was leaving for the Grand Canyon. His first question was which grand canyon. He knew more than one. When he realized I was going to the place we call Grand Canyon, he told a story.

"Long-time-ago," he said, "at the very beginning of things, there was only flat land where the Grand Canyon now lies. In that place lived the Male Waters and the Female Waters. There was a great conflict between them. The Male Waters were constantly striving to flow downwards, to move down, and the Female Waters were always trying to move upwards.

"This conflict brought about a great struggle between the two and eventually wore away a tremendous hole in the earth. Finally the Male Waters broke away and flowed to the sea. The Female Waters rose up as clouds and began drifting eastward, bringing rain across the Painted Desert and the Kaibito Plateau. When the clouds reached a sacred place called Black Mesa, they finally touched the earth again.

"But," he added, "Black Mesa is no longer sacred. White men have built roads and buildings there. The clouds are afraid to touch the earth anymore. The Female Waters no longer come. That is why it rains here very little now."

The following morning I said goodbye. Alice gave me some traveling bread made from blue corn, ground on a metate and mixed with juniper ash. As I walked out of the hogan, the old singer handed me a saddle blanket and said *"Hózhó nani-naadoo."* It was a traditional parting not used much anymore. Younger Navajo considered it old-fashioned. It meant "Go in beauty."

Only later did I learn about the Navajo idea of beauty and how it moves through life like a wind. It's not the beauty of surfaces alone, but an indwelling beauty that enfolds and completes, a life-restoring beauty. Only later did I learn about beauty and how it can be lost.

Redwall

After leaving the Navajo country earlier that spring, I took a job at Phantom Ranch in the canyon, working ten days on with four off. The ranch served as a base camp for exploring the inner canyon. A couple of months later I began guiding backpackers, working with my brother on his return from Mexico.

In the fall of the year, John and I began a long descent into the Grand Canyon. Following a break in the North Rim, two or three miles south of Point Imperial, we scrambled down a route I'd sketched on the map. Stands of fir and ponderosa screened the view of the gorge, but I could sense the vast emptiness lying unseen below.

Passing through the shadows of the rim forest, John and I descended the headwall of Nankoweap Canyon. We left the trees at the end of a promontory, breaking into the morning sunlight. Cliffs fell away, drop after sheer drop, into a deep immensity of rock and sky.

My brother took off his pack to adjust the load. Each of us carried water for two days and food for more than a week. This would take us through the first leg of the trip. Our needs had become elemental. I stood on the end of the point, looking.

Empty space drew the sky downward in a rush as bands of cliffs, running level for miles, pulled the field of vision wide. Vertical balanced horizontal. My brother put on his pack, and we stood there longer than needed, two figures suspended in a cliff-walled expanse.

We had stopped at the 8,000-foot level, a couple of thousand feet higher than the facing rim, nine miles away. The Colorado River flowed at the bottom of the gorge, a vertical mile below. I had measured these miles by the inch on the map, not by foot on the ground. The real distance, measured by time and effort, we still had to calculate.

Continuing lower, we carefully worked past cliffs and down debris slopes. It felt good to be moving. The physical push came as a release after weeks of sporadic preparations that increased in tempo as the trip approached. To the south, a faint ring of light circled the sun as it filtered through a scrim of cirrus clouds. Sun dogs glinted at each side, hinting of a coming storm. Expecting the normally clear weather for this time of year, we were traveling light without a tent or rain gear.

The Redwall, a massive limestone cliff 600 feet thick, formed a barrier below. Except for one point of weakness, the cliff curved unbroken along the canyonside. We angled to the head of a fault where the rock, stained an ocher red, had eroded into a steep chute. Sidestepping down to the bottom of the drainage, we left the fall weather behind and dropped into late summer.

Crossing from one dry fork of Nankoweap to another, we ended the first day camped deep in the rock stillness. Although conditioned by a summer of canyon hiking, we were tired. Scrambling with backpacks had been harder than anticipated, and I began to wonder if I'd underestimated the difficulty ahead.

The Grand Canyon is more than a single gorge. All the creeks and washes draining into the river have carved their own canyons. Branching and forking like the tines of an antler, they cut back into the plateau creating a maze of blind ravines and sunken streamways. Our plan was to take twenty-four days, hiking below the rim through the heart of the canyon system. Beginning at Nankoweap, we would traverse across twelve major canyons and dozens of nameless rifts to end in the upper Tapeats drainage.

The route I'd plotted on the map stayed high in the arterial canyons below the North Rim, keeping close to the Redwall. This meant gaining and losing considerable elevation each day as we crossed dividing ridges between drainages. I preferred this to following a more level course with long detours around the side canyons. If the route worked, it would shorten the distance considerably.

During the planning stage, I talked with legendary canyon hiker Harvey Butchart. The math professor provided detailed information on the terrain we wanted to cross, but advised me to keep closer to the river. He thought our intended route, although shorter, would be more difficult, drier, and less certain of success.

But I had something else in mind. The Redwall route, when plotted on the map, flowed in a graceful curve across the grain of the canyons. The line of the traverse wasn't perfect, but it was right.

That first evening, camped in the inner canyon, I studied the topo map. Tomorrow we planned to cross into Kwagunt, the next canyon south. A direct route passed through a saddle between Colter Butte and the rim, but no one had crossed it before. On the map, a line of sheer cliffs on the far side appeared impassable, but details can be lost in the scale of the map. Anything smaller than eighty feet, the contour interval, wasn't shown. The map might hide a barrier cliff, or a passage through one.

Next morning the band of sunlight widened on the rocks above. Using fuel tabs we heated cups of coffee laced Sherpa style with sugar, dried milk, and butter. We had planned our food down to the ounce with the proper amount of balanced calories needed for sustained effort. We took foods that didn't require cooking, freeing us from having to carry a stove and pot. Water was the heaviest item in our packs, but the consequences of running short far outweighed the extra load. We had pared our gear down to the essentials, wanting to move fast and light to cover the distance.

Hoisting our packs, we picked our way down the boulder-choked drainage. A chain of buttes ran along the dividing ridge to the south. Colter Butte sat directly above us on the line of the arc I wanted to follow. The high saddle west of it was tempting. But if it didn't go, we'd lose a day backtracking.

"Let's keep going down the drainage," John said. "It's the most logical route." Growing up, my brother had always taken the lead, being older and more aggressive. But a year of war had made a difference. He grew more cautious, and I found myself taking greater risks, balancing the equation. After talking over the options, he agreed to try the unclimbed saddle. We left the main drainage and headed up a branch.

Daylight had not reached to the bottom of the gorge. At a waterpocket in the bed of the Tapeats sandstone, my brother dropped on his stomach to drink. I scooped up a handful, the water cold on my teeth, before continuing up the steep incline. We had learned to drink whenever the chance came along.

Anticipation grew as we reached the narrow divide a couple of hours later. I pushed ahead and peered down the far side. Cliffs dropped 1,200 feet in stages to the canyon floor almost directly below. Our path was blocked. As John came up, I left my pack and scrambled down a chute to walk out the last possibility before turning back.

The break cut farther through the Redwall than it appeared from above. I worked down the rubble almost to the base of the limestone before being stopped by a cliff. A series of talus slopes covered the drops below it. This cliff was all that stood between us and the canyon bottom, but without a rope, I couldn't see a way to continue.

Carrying both packs, John met me at the bottom of the chute. "We have to turn back," I told him. "We can't get past the cliff." As I lifted my pack, he lowered his.

"Let me take a quick look," he said, disappearing behind a chockstone wedged between the walls. A moment later I heard him shout back, "It goes!"

The two of us descended a slot below the boulder. Reaching a narrow ledge, I faced the wall and sidestepped along the shelving rock to a way below. John lowered the packs with a cord before joining me at the foot of the cliff. We switchbacked down the high-angle talus into the Kwagunt drainage. That night, darkness overtook us in the Redwall narrows, forcing us to bivouac on a ledge.

As the days unfolded, we came to know the Redwall well as we searched for ways through its angular geometries. Reaching for handholds at times, I found fossils embedded in the rock—shells, plant stems, and sponges turned to chert nodules.

This was searock, formed in a still ocean, buried beneath thick sediments, uplifted, and finally wrenched into the hard light of the desert, 330 million years later and a mile higher than it started. Unbroken by major ledges, the single band of cliff meandered across the canyon wall, sweeping outward in spur-pointed curves. During one long day we passed through the Redwall four times.

Each morning we began moving when it was light enough to see and pushed until dark. We walked for miles beneath formations with names like Vishnu Temple, Wotans Throne, and Angels Gate. We walked all day, doing nothing else, sometimes walking for hours without a thought to show for it. Nearing our food cache at Phantom Ranch, the weather changed. Clouds thickened and lowered. A drenching rain came in the night at Clear Creek.

Awake before dawn, we packed our soggy gear and left at first light. When the sun broke over the rim, a wet heat rose skyward. We walked past the cliffs of Zoroaster Temple, across a plateau flecked with moving patches of light and shadow. The undulating terrace ended in a 1,500-foot trench cut into the ancient Precambrian rock by Bright Angel Creek. This was the primal Vishnu schist, squeezed beneath a range of mountains and recrystallized by pressured heat more than a billion and a half years ago.

Reaching the Kaibab Trail, a regular thoroughfare, we turned down the canyon to Phantom Ranch, an overnight stop for hikers and mule riders. The soft scent of fresh laundry drifted up-canyon. We passed through the cluster of boulder-footed cabins where dismounted riders were stretching stiff legs and rubbing sore haunches.

"These aren't so bad," John said, taking off a ripe pair of socks. We were sitting in the shower house. "They still have a couple of days' wear in them, but I'll test them anyway. If you throw a pair of socks against the wall and they stick, you know it's time to wash them."

He casually tossed a stiff sock against the opposite wall. It hit the rough-cut boards and stuck without moving. John stared for a moment at his hanging sock. "I guess it's time for a change," he said.

Originally we planned to lay over two nights at Phantom, but I didn't want to break the rhythm of the trip. We had reached the ranch several days ahead of schedule and were feeling strong. I wanted to keep walking, to keep the momentum going. We retrieved our food cache from the ranger and spread out the sleeping bags to dry.

Next day we headed up Bright Angel to the mouth of Phantom Canyon and entered the narrow gorge. Phantom Creek twisted between cliffs of gray Vishnu schist, veined by intrusions of red granite. As we rounded a bend, the clouds broke open and flooded the gorge in a wave of sudden light. Just as quickly they closed and left the canyon looking darker and more lifeless than before. We worked our way upstream, skirting deep plunge pools and spillways. The creek raced through the compound curves of the canyon, sunk too deep in the bedrock to reflect the sky.

We rounded a bend and found a twenty-foot waterfall blocking the canyon. I scrambled up a handhold climb, bypassing the falling stream. Once on top I pulled up the packs. After John joined me, we entered the open canyon above, walking through the layered sandstones and shales, broken by the pressures of shifting rock and widened by centuries of flowing water. Willow and arrowweed grew thick on the floodplain, while mesquite and catclaw took root on the drier slopes.

Late in the day, we reached the junction with Haunted Canyon and selected a fine overhang, protected from the rain and away from rising waters. Setting down my pack, I cleared a spot for the night. Making camp when traveling light had become second nature, done without thought. Unfold a thin pad and shake out an even thinner sleeping bag. Camp was ready.

With some daylight remaining, I walked up Haunted Canyon, following the main flow to the source of the creek. Water gushed from green layers of Bright Angel shale, breaking into the light of day. A couple of years before, it had fallen as rain on the North Rim, percolating down through 3,000 feet of rock. To the east rose a towering butte named Buddha Temple, to the south Isis, and to the west the sky island of Shiva. Surrounded by temples and shrines, I saw only rock and sky. It was enough.

Back at camp, the night slowly welled up from the bottom of

the canyon, filling the void. Thoughts drifted and the surface of things faded. Bats flickered in the dark sky as I leaned back in the overhang and listened. The rain had ended, but the creek still moved, spilling over rock in a murmur older than words. John also sat listening, thinking about something.

At dawn we walked to the head of Phantom in a gray light, thickened by rain. The route led up tiered cliffs on the worn face of the Redwall. Heavy clouds spilled over the rim, dissolving as they fell into frayed patches and tendrils of smoky mist. We climbed the rock, exposed and crumbling under hand and foot, crossed a high saddle, and descended into the gullet of Dragon Creek.

A flash flood caught us the next day. We heard a high, steady rush like the sound of wind moving through the trees. It came from somewhere up-canyon. Realizing floodwaters were on their way, we climbed to higher ground and waited. The sound continued undiminished but nothing appeared. We kept waiting. Water in a dry country moves like blood through the veins. It comes in pulses, flood one moment and drought the next. Sometimes a flash flood appears as a wall of water tearing down a dry wash. Sometimes it doesn't. At last a thick tongue of water snaked down the creekbed, a flood without much flash.

We grabbed our packs and walked next to the leading edge of the flood as it meandered down the gorge. Our pace carried us along faster than the flow of water. We pulled ahead for a time, but when we stopped to rest the flash flood caught up.

Rain fell all day. By the time we sought shelter for the night, we had entered the Precambrian rock, lying several formations below the Redwall and deposited more than a billion years before it. The Colorado River, carving through the Precambrian rock, formed the Inner Gorge. This deep canyon within a canyon had few overhangs.

But at dusk I spotted a horizontal crack wide enough for two. Pushing in on my back, I cleared out the spider webs. The ceiling pressed a couple of inches above my face, so close I couldn't roll over. No matter, it was dry. Falling asleep, I listened as the rush of water turned into a swallowed roar.

By dawn we found ourselves on the wrong side of a creek in

full flood. Mud-thick water churned through the gorge. Boulders rolled unseen below the surface, crashing together with hollow clacks. To continue our trek, we had to cross.

Scouting upstream we found a narrows where the creek funneled through a slot. A log, wedged against rocks, half-spanned the flood. The water flowed deep and fast. I didn't like the look of it, but it was the best crossing we could find. Keeping our packs on, we unbuckled the waist straps in case of a slip.

Wet but stable, the log took us to mid-creek without trouble. I glanced ahead and leaped over the deepest channel before I had time to think about it. Bouncing off a boulder, I landed on the far side, dragging a boot in the water but ending upright. John followed and we climbed toward a break in the cliffs leading onto the Tonto Plateau.

Crossing the broad bench, we skirted the deep gorge of Tuna Creek. To the west curved Scorpion Ridge, the great bulk of Mencius Butte stood to the east, and Point Sublime, cloud-hidden, rose somewhere above. Normally a desert, the Tonto had turned into a bog. Water flowed in rivulets down each wash. We passed mushrooms growing next to cactus and we slogged ahead with mud clinging to boots and clothes hanging wet and heavy. We talked little, drawn into ourselves by the weather.

Descending a break in the Tapeats sandstone, we crossed the head of the creek, running full. John noticed a large overhang at the base of the cliff above us and went to check it out. "It's dry," he shouted.

The weather brought with it an early twilight, so the decision to stop early came easily. Everything we carried was wet, and whenever we stopped walking we began to shiver. Unpacking, we spread out our gear and built a small drying fire from brushwood.

After taking care of our immediate needs, we took a closer look at our surroundings and realized we had camped in a shelter used since prehistoric times. Centuries before someone had packed fill dirt behind a terrace wall to widen the natural ledge into a platform. Ash and charcoal from old campfires had blackened the wet slope below the shelter. Mixed into it were bits of broken pottery and rainwashed flakes of stone.

As it grew dark, John described a troubling dream he had the night before. In it he found himself floating high above the earth, a single point in a universe structured with crystalline perfection. The whole was so precariously balanced, it frightened him. A slight nudge at the wrong point and it could all collapse, falling in upon itself.

Next morning I pulled on boots still wet and began gathering gear that was only half-dry. Yesterday's fire had burned to fine ash, which I scooped up and tossed into the creek. I wanted to remove all traces of our camp. As I began to scatter the unused pieces of firewood, John stopped me. "I'll take care of it," he said.

He took the few remaining sticks and piled them at the foot of the cliff in the driest section of the overhang. "Somebody might come along and need a fire some day."

Four days later we switchbacked up the head of Crazy Jug Canyon, a branch of Tapeats Creek. We reached the North Rim and entered the open light of the plateau where the sky spread wide above the trees. By now our packs had become so much a part of us, we didn't bother to take them off to rest. Lean and weather-hardened, we left behind the Grand Canyon, having completed the trip in under two weeks.

We stood on the canyon rim, looking back, gazing into a place of improbable beauty. Cliff walls fell away one after the other, dropping into the haze, falling into deeper canyons, disappearing into the farther distance. No end to it.

We called this the end of the trip, but it was only a shift in directions. After this, the course of our lives veered apart, taking different paths.

No Man

Few words pass between Scott Milzer and me as snow falls through the nightsky, blowing steadily. We are following an endless highway west of Paria Plateau. I stare ahead trying to see the road as flakes stream past the windshield, hypnotically, the way stars on the big screen pass by at warp speed. "Another space odyssey," Milzer says.

Drive through a dark snowstorm and the desert transforms into something light years away from home ground. The road disappears ahead, absorbed by the flat wall of night. Whether it's ascending or descending, I can't tell. Burntwater lies behind us, but we need to find a place to wait out the storm before continuing.

As we drift along the highway, I ask Milzer about his girlfriend. He hasn't mentioned her yet. "We broke up a few months ago," he tells me.

She was acting moody one day, he says, when he casually suggested they take a break from each other. She agreed with more enthusiasm than he expected. "The next time she called was to tell me she was getting married."

Ahead the road drops through a hole in the storm, entering a pocket of diffused light coming from Fredonia, population 1,200 and falling. The snow ceases abruptly on the outskirts of town. "This place is so small," Milzer says, "it doesn't even have its own weather."

Stopping at a pay phone, I call Tony Williams, who moved to this small town to be halfway between Zion and the Grand Canyon, the two centers of his world. He was part of our changing circle of friends whose numbers always stayed around thirty, about the size of an ice-age hunting band. "No problem," he says when I ask if he can put us up for the night.

We find Tony's double-wide on a back street. Inside, he's reading the *Wall Street Journal* and listening to the BBC on the shortwave. Once married, Tony now lives alone. On the wall hangs a map of Zion. Books on the Utah wilderness lie on a table with a biography of T. E. Lawrence. Tony once retraced Lawrence of Arabia's route through the Wadi Rum and spent several nights camped surreptitiously in the rock-carved city of Petra. Next to the biography sits a new translation of the *Iliad*. The original version in ancient Greek lies within reach so he can check its accuracy.

Homer's epic reminds me of a question I have concerning Everett Ruess, a young artist who disappeared in the canyon country in the 1930s. He was reading the *Odyssey* at the time. Milzer and I are planning to hike into Davis Gulch to his last campsite. One of the only clues he left behind was the word "Nemo" carved on a canyon wall.

"What's Nemo mean?" I ask Tony, an occasional river guide trained in the classics. He stands at the stove preparing an Ilam tea brought back from Nepal the year before.

"Nemo is actually a Latin translation of the Greek word, *oudeis*," he says. "It was the name Odysseus used to trick the Cyclops and escape from his cave. It means, 'no man'."

The sound of the word, spoken in the dead tongue of Homer, makes me curious. When I ask Tony if he knows any passages in ancient Greek, he begins reciting a few lines from memory. Not knowing the meaning of the words, I hear their rhythmic flow as an incantation, a voice surfacing from the past.

"One thing for sure," Milzer adds, "Homer wasn't a sailor. If he was, Odysseus would have showed up at home with a pile of dirty laundry and a hard-on."

Before turning in we make plans for the next day. Tony says we'll need at least a day for the roads to dry before trying to reach Davis Gulch. Meanwhile the three of us will head to Zion, taking a back road if the weather clears.

Sitting at the kitchen table early the next morning, I study the topos. Contour lines tighten along the Virgin River, marking the great cliffs of Zion. The rhythm of the topography plays out in my head as I scan a map. At some point it becomes a meditation, the eye taking as long to move across the terrain as it takes the foot to walk it.

Pulling myself away, I get up to make another cup of coffee and ask Milzer if he wants one. "Yes," he says, although he hasn't touched his first. "I always like a cup of coffee sitting next to me getting cold."

Tony comes in from outside, striding with purpose as he pieces together his own weather report. He has synthesized the late-night TV weather from Salt Lake City that he taped, a brief radio update from southern Utah, and finally a look at the sky itself. Although he lives in Arizona, he can't get a state weather report. It's impossible for him to pick up an Arizona radio or TV station and no one in town sells an Arizona newspaper. Normally he doesn't find the isolation to be a handicap.

"It doesn't look good," he announces, "and another front is moving in tomorrow evening."

With a new storm coming, we need to take advantage of the drier weather. We pile into the truck and head west. Stormclouds circle the horizon leaving a lens of blue sky above us. The highway runs straight across the broad benchlands lying between the Grand Canyon to the south and a series of cliffs stair-stepping northward into Utah.

As we drive down an almost empty highway, I brief Tony on our plans for the next few days. If the weather cooperates, we'll hike into Davis, drive across the Aquarius Plateau, and then swing through the homeland of the prehistoric Anasazi Indians. He might join us for the backcountry portion, he says, but will pass on the ruins.

"After Thebes, Luxor, and the Parthenon, Anasazi sites are all pretty meager," Tony says, smiling at the thought. "Just a few pitiful potsherds."

"When did the Anasazi invent the potsherd, anyway?" Milzer wonders.

Beyond Pipe Springs, the Vermilion Cliffs press close to the highway. Crossing a juniper-studded ridge, the highway drops toward Short Creek and the clustered homes of Colorado City, an enclave of several thousand polygamists. Although not sanctioned by the Church of Jesus Christ of the Latter-day Saints, they consider themselves true Mormons.

A sandstone escarpment, rising into the truncated pinnacles of Canaan Mountain, shelters the town that straddles the Arizona-Utah border. Early residents nailed skids to the bottoms of the first houses they built in case they needed to pull them across the state line to avoid the authorities.

The fundamentalist sect remains sternly Old Testament in outlook. Boys dress in western shirts buttoned at the neck and girls wear gingham dresses over long pants. Many of them hold the belief that at the moment Jesus died on the cross the earth split open in a great earthquake, forming the Grand Canyon.

Disowned by the official Mormon church, members of the community claim to be the spiritual descendants of the prophets Joseph Smith and Brigham Young. The town's inhabitants continue to practice their teachings on plural marriage, although the church prohibited polygamy a century ago.

"Polygyny," Tony reminds me, "is the more accurate term since a man is allowed multiple wives but a woman can marry only a single husband."

The Short Creekers live outside laws no longer taken seriously. The last attempt to enforce the anti-polygamy laws occurred in 1953 when the governor of Arizona secretly declared that a state of insurrection existed in their community. State police and FBI agents raided the settlement under the darkness of a total eclipse.

Approaching with car lights off, the posse hesitated when locals set off a few sticks of dynamite buried in the road. No one was hurt. Continuing into the community, they arrested a couple of dozen men and rounded up the women and children. But when word of the raid reached the newspapers, opinion turned against the governor and cost him his re-election bid.

As we cross into Utah, passing homes with more than one front door, I wonder about marriage taken in large doses. Of the three of us, I'm the only one still married. "Why would you want to have sixteen wives simultaneously?" I wonder.

"The road of excess leads to the palace of wisdom," Milzer says.

"William Blake," Tony adds.

"Blake?" asks Milzer. "I thought I was quoting Brigham Young."

A few miles past Colorado City, we turn off the highway onto a dirt road that skirts Smithsonian Butte on a shortcut to Zion. Ruts, sunk deep into the red mud, have dried near the highway, but the road grows softer the farther we drive. Dodging a few deep mud holes, we pass a spot where several vehicles have turned around leaving a starburst of tracks. I figure they were left by locals who know the road. But the realization that it's the point of no return doesn't hit until a moment later when the road suddenly transforms into pure gumbo.

Sticky mud coats the tires with thick adobe retreads that reduce braking and steering to almost nothing. The road takes a slight dip. The truck coasts along at only five miles an hour, but I can't bring it to a stop as it slowly glides toward the ditch. That doesn't worry me. What does, lies around the next bend where the road drops steeply downward on the edge of a deep ravine. Even in dry weather this stretch forces you to pay attention.

"The road gets worse up ahead," I say as the truck comes to a stop at a skewed angle in the middle of the road. "We won't make it."

Unable to go forward, turn around, or back up, I sit thinking as Milzer recounts details of the latest Third World bus plunge. All we can do is try pushing. My friends work their way through the mud to the front of the truck. As soon as they push, their feet slide out from under them. But I notice the truck has moved laterally a few inches and cut the wheels as far as they will turn. Tony now shoves sideways from the driver's side, and Milzer pushes in the opposite direction from the rear. To our surprise, the truck spins smoothly around until it points back the way we came. Both of the pushers jump on the tailgate, giving me just enough traction to move forward. I keep the momentum going until we reach a drier stretch within sight of Duttons Pass. If we can't enter Zion, at least we'll get a look at it.

Leaving the truck, we start walking toward the pass, a low saddle between Smithsonian Butte and Canaan Mountain. After covering a mile or two, the three of us scramble up the last few hundred feet. A stand of juniper screens the view as we work our way to the north side of the pass.

In 1880 geologist Clarence Dutton rode horseback to the top of the overlook and stopped, stunned by the rock expanse spread out before him. He gazed across at the massive Towers of the Virgin, the gateway to what is now Zion National Park. In time, the geologist believed, this view would be recognized as one of the finest in the world. More than a century has passed and few of those who know about it have made the trek.

For many nineteenth-century travelers, an obsession with viewpoints became a way to distance themselves from nature. But Dutton was different. He came here to experience the natural world as a whole, to absorb it in all its wild complexity. To do that he needed perspective. The right perch helped.

A few steps more and we emerge into the open light. Across the Virgin River the rock faces of Zion tower thousands of feet higher than the canyon floor. Immense sandstone walls climb above layers of redrock to end in pure dentate peaks. Cliffrock undulates up both sides of the main gorge as it cuts back into the snow-covered plateau. A mass of disturbed clouds surges above the skyline like some long-dormant force beginning to awaken.

Below us, the branches of the Virgin join together to flow westward. At the confluence, Zion Canyon meets the gorge of the Parunuweap, a Paiute name with a sound as hollow and resonant as drum beats. Duttons Pass, where we stand, merges with the sheer-cut face of Canaan Mountain, curving to the north. It's a land without gradations where clifftop drops sheer to cliff bottom, a land described by an early settler as a "jumping-off place at world's end."

The three of us turn away from Dutton's perch and backtrack toward the truck. "The most dangerous animal on the Colorado Plateau is not a rattlesnake or scorpion," Tony tells us as we walk. "It's the red ant." He recounts the times he's been bitten between the toes and on the soft under-flesh of the upper arm. "Those bastards are vicious."

"Well, I'll admit they're bad," says Milzer, "but in my book the red chile is more dangerous."

"Chile peppers are good for you, though."

"How can it be good for you to have your mouth and stomach lining burned?"

" 'Good for you,' " Tony admits, "is perhaps not the right choice of words. But it feels good when it stops."

A dozen cows have congregated around the pickup in our absence. One is rubbing against the side mirror; the others stand waiting for us to feed them, looking dully expectant.

"Can you imagine spending your life as a cowboy serving these beasts?" asks Tony as he climbs into the truck.

"You could do worse," says Milzer.

On the drive back to Fredonia, I suggest heading to No Mans Mesa, north of Kanab. I noticed it on the map that morning.

"It's definitely worth seeing," Tony says. "But you won't make it there in this, even if the road's dry." Although preferring to walk, he finds his low-geared, four-wheel-drive Blazer useful on the backroads. He checks his watch. "We might have enough time, if we take my truck."

Transferring vehicles in Fredonia, we head northeast, following a line of cliffs past Hells Bellow. We have sixty miles ahead of us, the last twenty on sandy roads. Already past noon, we'll be cutting it close to get back by dark. We turn onto a dirt road and enter a breach in the vertical rock, moving as fast as washouts and mudholes permit.

The Blazer rattles up the main wash as Tony questions Milzer about the fishing business. Each spring he goes to sea swearing it will be his last trip, but another Seattle winter comes along and he finds himself packing his sea bags once again. Tony wants to know how a gill netter operates. The fisherman gives him a quick rundown on the risks and profits. "There's not much to it," he adds. "The net goes out, the net comes in."

Milzer turns the tables, asking Tony what he does for a living. It's an awkward question since Tony doesn't work. At one point in his life he realized if he lived frugally and was careful with his investments he could get by without a job. So he chose not to work.

"You can imagine the inner turmoil each time someone asks what I do," says Tony. "In our society a person's identity and sense of worth are based on the type of work he does. I don't work." After pausing a moment, he adds with a smile, "I guess you'd call me Oudeis. Call me No Man."

The road leaves the drainage and finds a passage through the caprock to the tablelands above. The terrain opens to the north giving us our first view of No Mans Mesa. Unbroken cliffs of Navajo sandstone rise from a pediment as smooth and white as bone. The upper cliffs appear unscalable without climbing gear, but Tony knows a route up the north face.

Soon the road tops a rise and sinks again. A lone butte of white sandstone curves upward, capped by a nubbin of red-rock. It appears for only a moment, but there's no mistaking the legendary Mollies Nipple. The place name frequently turns up in southern Utah, but the identity of Mollie remains uncertain. Some credit rancher John Kitchen for naming the original butte after his wife, but the name appeared on maps before he brought his bride here in 1879.

The road descends steeply down a sand slope into a narrow basin, skirting a ranch house. Finding the right turn, we plow through deep sand into the North Swag. A few junipers grow above a sagebrush thicket reaching higher than the truck. Tony is getting a workout, constantly swinging the steering wheel back and forth to dodge brush and stay on course.

A dusting of snow clings to a few ledges on the sheer north face of No Mans. The cliff line flows upward in a bold sweep of Navajo sandstone. At the head of the swag, the old road climbs a steep slickrock divide. Tony guns the truck up the first pitch and parks on a landing barely wide enough to turn around.

Continuing on foot, we pass a weathered cow skull with a gaping hole punched in the front. "That's the type of wound Homer described at the siege of Troy," Tony says as he inspects the damage.

We reach the foot of the route and work our way up a cone of talus, covering the lower cliff. A patch of snow holds the tracks of a bobcat that earlier followed the same route. Remnants of a trail pick up where the talus ends, zigzagging up the ledges. A rancher built the route to the mesatop when he needed a place to hide his herd of goats from the banker.

Once on the summit of the sky island, we cross the untracked surface. Soft under foot, the rippling sand holds the shape of old winds. Beyond a fringe of stunted ponderosa pines spreads an unbroken cover of piñon and juniper. The quiet of the trees absorbs our conversation, even the sound of walking doesn't break the silence. Soon each of us wanders off in a different direction.

In a sandy pocket among the trees I come across a prehistoric camp. Chunks of fire-cracked rock lie mixed with translucent flakes of chalcedony. I pick up a small flake, retouched along the edge by a toolmaker centuries ago. Stress lines radiate from the point of impact where a single, sharp blow from another stone sent the chip flying. Whoever sat here knapping on rocks had the idea of a tool in mind before beginning. The idea led step by step from the raw stone to the finished tool, from the present to the future, drawing the toolmaker into the flow of time. I run my thumb down the sharp edge and over the smooth, rounded bulge. It has a human feel to it, a stone shaped to match a thought.

A lone raven turns above the rim of No Mans Mesa. Nothing moves below. I stand on the edge looking down upon a deep expanse of rock and desert trees. No map labels this a wilderness; it isn't necessary. The moment itself lies untracked, pristine, and we are part of it. Even at night we are contained by it. Drifting to sleep, we are enclosed by dreams of gnarled junipers under a sky of empty blue.

Night pulls away from the horizon revealing a sky, cloudless and drained of color. The slate wiped clean. Absolution, for the moment.

Before the next storm can overtake us, we hurriedly load the vehicles and leave for Davis Gulch in the Escalante River country. Scott and I ride in one truck, following Tony in the other. We take the highway north of town to avoid another long shortcut. If the weather holds we'll follow an elliptic route to the southeast corner of Utah and eventually into New Mexico. Soon a beat-up truck approaches from the opposite direction with kayak on top and a cow skull mounted on the hood.

"Cabeza de Vaca," Milzer says, referring to the survivor of a failed Spanish expedition to Florida in 1528. Familiar with each other's way of thinking, our conversations are often compressed into a string of impressions, each triggered by a single word or phrase. My friend sits without further comment as an image gathers of a man walking barefoot across America to become the first European to enter the Southwest. Truck and cow skull shrink in the rearview mirror as we turn east.

Our two-truck caravan skirts Bryce Canyon and drives through Tropic, a ranch town gathered together, Mormon-style, on the headwaters of the Paria River. Instead of living in isolated ranches, Mormon cowboys built their homes in town and commuted to the range. A cattleman from here, Wallace Ott, once told me about meeting Everett Ruess, not long before Ruess disappeared. The young man passed through Tropic in the fall of 1934 with his two burros and a string of questions. He asked Wallace about the region's history, saying he planned to do some writing.

Several years before, Everett had left California and hitchhiked to the canyon country in search of beauty. He kept returning, and his travels grew increasingly dreamlike. At times he realized his life had become impossibly strange and unreal. "I have seen almost more beauty," he once wrote, "than I can bear."

After leaving Tropic, Everett took the Hole-in-the-Rock Road south of Escalante and camped on what he called the rim of the world. The next day he continued south, writing in his last letter, "Nothing stands between me and the wild."

When the rancher next heard about Everett, the young dreamer had disappeared in the maze of slickrock canyons near Hole-in-the-Rock. In the winter of 1935 a search party from Escalante trailed into Davis Gulch, Everett's last known camp. The horsemen scanned the cliffs for signs of the artist who had entered this canyon a few months before.

The searchers located Everett's base camp and found his burros fending for themselves. Pushing deeper, they came upon the last clue to his disappearance. Carved in his hand on the wall of an Anasazi ruin was the name NEMO. He had been reading T. E. Lawrence's translation of the *Odyssey* so may have borrowed the name from Homer. Everett vanished, as if swallowed by the rock itself. He once had written, "When I go, I leave no trace."

A Navajo story, told within the Nightway chant, traces the journey of a boy called The Dreamer. As night overtakes him in a canyon, the Holy People appear in the form of four bighorn sheep. He lifts his bow but cannot shoot, and the bighorn become his guides. After many adventures, he returns to teach his brother the Nightway ceremony. Finally The Dreamer rises in the sky and disappears into a cliff face where the rock opens like a door.

We pull into Escalante and stop at a gas station before taking the Hole-in-the-Rock Road. The name comes from an epic Mormon expedition that cut a wagon road through the cliffs to the south in 1879. "If you go out to Hole-in-the-Rock," the attendant tells us as he runs a squeegee across the windshield, "be sure to get back tonight. There's a storm coming."

Climbing into the truck I wonder how he can pump the gas, check the oil, wash the windows—and still charge less than a self-serve station in the city. "It's a loss leader," Milzer says. "He makes up for it on towing charges when you get stuck down that dirt road sixty miles from town."

A pair of ravens fly overhead as we turn south toward Hole-in-the-Rock. "Ravens are just too damn smart for their bodies," Milzer says, watching their aerobatics out the window. "Always bored. It gets them into trouble, just like people. No one believes me but I once saw a raven swing completely upside down on a wire, let loose, then do a somersault and catch the wire beneath it."

Following us on this stretch, Tony keeps close enough to maintain visual contact. After rattling down the road for a couple of hours, I downshift into first gear as the truck noses into the deep cut of Carcass Wash. The grade is steep, the road narrow and rutted, and extremely slick in wet weather. Years ago a busload of Boy Scouts took a plunge into this ravine during a downpour. At the head of Davis Gulch not far beyond, we back the trucks off the road and make camp. Next we search for a level spot to toss out our bags as a front noses over the western uplands, compressing the sky under a thick slab of cloud.

The morning sun bellies over the horizon, a pale yellow disk dimming to gray as it lifts into the cloud cover. To take even a quick look at the canyon where Everett disappeared might mean getting snowed in for several days. After weighing the risks of being stranded so far from a paved road, I decide to chance it.

Wind picks up as the three of us walk cross-country at a fast clip. The low ceiling and flat light make it hard to judge the distance. Two hours, I guess, to reach the trailhead. Buffeted by a crosswind, we traverse a barren expanse of sandstone humps and hollows, folding together as smoothly as sea waves. An open parka frames Milzer's T-shirt, printed with "The Wreck of the Lady Mary," one of his own paintings. He can't believe we're going ahead with this.

"Another mad skipper," he says, just loud enough for me to

hear. A gust throws him off his stride. Then he shouts to Tony above the wind. "I've resigned myself to being marooned out here for a couple of days."

"I warn you, Milzer," Tony calls back. "Don't let Scott do your thinking for you. The worst case out here can be far worse than being stranded for two days."

Locating the way into the gorge takes longer than expected; we don't recognize the route until we're on top of it. Finding the blind trail, the three of us zigzag down a steep face, following a narrow sill cut into the slickrock. The trickling of hidden water rises from below. Once on the canyon floor, we find an inscription carved by one of the men who searched for Ruess. It reads "Mar. 6 Walter Allen 1935."

When the search party returned without finding Everett, rumors circulated that he had been murdered by rustlers. Others suggested he staged his own disappearance, slipping across the Colorado River into the Navajo country. But the most likely possibility is that he died in a fall. He was known to scale cliffs with a recklessness that unnerved those watching him.

Evidence surfaced in the mid-1970s to support the theory of a climbing accident. An unidentified Californian was motoring across Lake Powell when he waved down a Park Service boat. He handed the ranger, Roe Barney, a sack of bones and told him he had just returned from Davis Gulch where he had been looking for Indian ruins. Near the rim of the canyon he spotted a skeleton wedged deep within a crack in the rock. He roped down to it and found signs of a broken hip and collar bone. Leaving most of the remains in place, he removed a few bones for identification.

The ranger, who grew up in Escalante, immediately suspected they might be the remains of Everett Ruess. When he returned to park headquarters he handed over the human bones to a supervisor. Unfortunately they disappeared. Rangers have since searched their holdings and records without finding either the bones or information on where they were found.

"I plan to be on my way back by noon, and even that's taking a chance," Tony says with an eye on the threatening sky. Stormclouds surge across the gap between the rims as we split into two parties. Tony heads down canyon, Milzer and I turn up, planning to meet later.

The gorge loops back and forth like a tangled rope. Beaver have dammed the creek, filling the canyon floor with a string of pools. Willow thickets choke the banks; scrub oaks grow on the higher terraces. Sheer canyon walls curve around us as if smoothed by hand. We follow a bighorn trail, traversing sandy slopes above the creek, and reach a natural arch standing a hundred feet high. The massive sandstone buttress curves down from the canyon rim. Wind whips through the opening as we turn back, already short on time.

Close to where the trail enters the gorge, we pass Everett's old campsite in a shallow alcove at the base of a cliff. Remnants of a 1,000-year-old pictograph, the white pigments of a headdress and necklace, cover the rock face above. Nothing else remains of the archaic figure; the human form has faded away, ghostlike. No man.

Rain begins to fall as we leave the rock art panel and reach the foot of the trail. The only sign of Tony is a cairn he left as a pre-arranged signal to let us know he had returned to camp. "That was fast," Milzer says. "He must have run around the corner and waited until we left. That's what I would have done, only I packed my gear on the wrong truck."

We push hard without pausing to rest, taking the full brunt of the storm head-on. "It's no use, captain," Milzer says, bending into the cold wind, "I can't hold her."

Flecks of snow fly past in quick bursts. The force of the storm is building. Reaching camp, we find only one truck. Tony has left. A wiperblade holds a note on the windshield of the pickup, but gale force winds snatch it from my hand before I can read it. The paper flies away, high above the ground, a message never received.

Bouncing along the road at the foot of the Straight Cliffs, we make it past Carcass and a series of deep washes beyond. The road is wet but still gives good traction. It won't last long. Cold air cascades down the wall of the plateau to the west, carrying wisps of snow that evaporate in the dry air before touching the ground. By the time we reach a graded stretch of road, the snow is beginning to stick.

Friends of mine once spent several days backpacking across the rim country above the Escalante River. Miles from road or trail, they came upon a single set of boot tracks, worn smooth and heading directly toward a slot canyon. They followed the tracks to a hidden spring where the man had knelt down to drink. He left by the same route. Whoever it was knew the country well.

"Everett Ruess is still out here," Milzer says, after hearing the story, "and he doesn't even know he's missing."

Snow covers the slickrock and sand, catching in the branches of blackbrush as it falls. Clouds settle over the mesas and far mountains, obscuring landmarks and drawing down an early dusk.

By the time the two of us reach the highway, the truck is cutting deep tracks in the snow. Rimmed by high country, we'll get snowed in at Escalante unless we take a chance and push on. No sign of Tony. Days later we learn he returned safely to Fredonia. We turn east into the thick of the storm, heading toward the Aquarius Plateau. One section rises more than 11,000 feet, making it the highest plateau in North America. If we cross a lower corner before the storm closes the highway, we should be able to work our way slowly into New Mexico.

Reaching the town of Boulder, Utah, we stop at a small grocery store, the only place still open. An antique cash register sits on a counter next to a pair of scales with a few canned goods lining the back shelves. Behind the counter stands a cowboy, with graying hair and a red flannel shirt, holding a yellowed copy of *The Reader's Digest* in one hand and a magnifying glass in the other. He nods as we enter and goes back to his reading, working his lips silently as he moves down the page, word by word. He's missing a couple of digits on one hand; his face is scarred and weather-cured. The old cowboy doesn't look up until we leave.

"If you head up the mountain," he warns in a voice meant to be taken seriously, "be careful."

"I wish he hadn't said that," Milzer says as we return to the truck.

Angling into the storm, the road switchbacks sharply up Boulder Mountain, a portion of the Aquarius Plateau to the north. Deep drifts have blocked one side, narrowing the pavement to a single lane. But we have it all to ourselves; no one has come down the mountain for some time. Visibility deteriorates, forcing us to slow to a crawl; traction lessens in the deepening snow. We'll have to turn back if it gets any worse, but there's nowhere to turn around. With both hands gripping the wheel, I hold to the road as it climbs steadily. Finally, at 9,200 feet, it tips the other direction and we find ourselves heading downhill on the far side of the mountain. We soon break out of the storm, surprised to have made it across.

Within a mile or two the snowcover thins, turning to slush on the roadway. Farther north, the sun bores through the stormclouds in a shaft of burning light, a column of fire. Entering Capitol Reef National Park, we pass an "Orientation Pullout."

"Sometimes," Milzer says, glancing at the sign, "a little disorientation is what you need to appreciate this place."

The two-lane highway follows the Fremont River as it cleaves through the great flex of the Waterpocket Fold. Erosion has cut and scoured wide swaths, leaving others untouched. These remnants rise as massive buttes and temples. Stormlight hits the whaleback ridges above, fading here and reappearing there, moving in pulses across the massive sandstone cliffs. In a flash of revelation, it illuminates an isolated rockform for only a moment before disappearing.

Familiar with an artist's palette, Milzer observes the changing tones of the rock. "Fugitive," he says. "That's what you'd have to call these colors. Painters avoid fugitive colors. The pigments fade over time like that pictograph at Everett's camp." He looks across the rockscape at the shifting reds and sandy whites. "In the desert we're all fugitive—the painter and his colors."

At Hanksville, a desert crossroads with a population of a few hundred, we park in front of Shirley's Rock Shop. The walls have been built with chunks of petrified wood and fossil-laden stone. Inside, proprietor Ernest Shirley leans on the counter in his Big Mac coveralls, his hair brush-cut and flecked with gray. A pair of glasses, missing one lens, perches on the end of his nose as he studies a specimen.

This high desert country draws a mix of people. Those with no connection to their surroundings could live anywhere. Others have become trapped here, unable to leave. Then there are those like Ernie who have been selected by a place, becoming as much a part of the scenery as the rocks themselves.

Dinosaur bone and petrified wood crowd the shelves. Potsherds fill cardboard boxes; display cases hold arrowheads and the rarer fossils. Milzer hunts through a box of sliced and polished coprolites, dinosaur turds. He wants to find the right one to make into a bola tie. Ernie places the dinosaur claw he was examining into a drawer and gently slides it shut, inviting us to take a look at his prize Allosaur bone in the workshop out back.

The three of us weave through a yard filled with mounds of agate and obsidian, fossil bone, strange concretions, and geological anomalies. We pass stone, raw and rough-cut, polished and tumbled, sorted in bins and piles. Ernie leads us to the dinosaur femur, an immense bone about six feet long. He found the fossil, broken in two, north of town. With the help of three men and a come-along, he lowered it down a cliff face and wheelbarrowed it two miles to his truck. He tells us that every dinosaur expert in the world has passed through here. "I've talked to sixty of 'em, and they all tell me something different."

Back in the shop, he mentions that the uranium mined for the first atomic bomb came from Temple Mountain to the north. In the 1950s, he adds, prospectors searched for high-grade ore concentrated in fossils and petrified wood. I ask him if he's ever passed a Geiger counter over his collection to check for radiation. "No," he says, unconcerned about the risk. "If it didn't kill Andrew Hunt, I guess it's not going to kill me."

Hunt, he explains, was the first uranium miner in history. He worked at a mine in Disappointment Valley, Colorado, where Madame Curie came to buy her ore. Upon retiring, he moved to Hanksville. "He lived until ninety years old," Ernie says, "when his son backed over him in the driveway. Still didn't kill him. They put him in a nursing home but he ran away and lived five more years."

I turn a potsherd to catch the window light, examining the black-on-white pattern. "Cowboys found lots of pots in the old days," Ernie says. "The ones that were too big to pack out they tossed over the cliff for fun, just like cowboys. They thought they would always be there."

Hanksville once served as a way station for Butch Cassidy and the Wild Bunch. They used the Robbers Roost country, across the Dirty Devil River, as a hideout. Many inhabitants of southern Utah still consider Cassidy a local hero. I ask the fossil hunter for his opinion of the outlaw.

"Butch Cassidy wasn't any different from lots of others," he tells me. "Back in those days you can't tell outlaws from ones that weren't. They'd steal horses and run 'em across the Dirty Devil. Those on this side would go over there and steal horses on that side and run 'em back. Butch just grabbed him some horses and started riding. But when you run with the wolves," he adds, "you become a wolf."

Bone-tired, we leave Shirley's rock pile. It's getting too late to push on and find a camp, so we put up at the only motel still open this time of year. Tomorrow we'll backpack into one of Butch Cassidy's old haunts along the Dirty Devil River, giving the weather another day to clear. We take a room where sand drifts under the hollow core door onto a worn carpet. The tap water never gets above lukewarm. I lie staring at the ceiling, listening to the wind sweep away the last hours of the day.

Time slows, becoming more tangible, almost solid. In rain country the organic cycle of growth and decay shapes the sense of duration. But here in the arid West it's different. Time is more geologic than biologic. It accumulates, layer upon layer, incrementally slow until all at once the pattern reverses. A tremendous rock slab suddenly unhinges, crashing from a cliff face; a flash flood rushes down an arroyo without warning. Ripping through the strata, erosion lays open the past, exposing the raw edges of history.

Dawn finds Milzer and me back in the truck, punching through sand drifts on a backroad south of Hanksville. It winds like a dry river through the wider expanse. Behind us, snow blankets the high-angle profile of the Henry Mountains, adding to their sense of remoteness. The Henrys were the last mountains to be mapped in the continental United States. Skirting Hell Hole Swale we reach the head of Angel Trail, Butch Cassidy's escape route to Robbers Roost.

Below us, the river has excavated a trench through the sandstone. Slickrock domes and canyon walls form a sunken corridor bordering the Burr Desert. The shallow winter light falls on the rock, drawing out the reds and spectral whites.

At the trailhead we repack our gear and descend a clearly

marked trail. But once through the caprock, the route fades as it crosses a bald sandstone face. Cairns strung along the route don't help. No matter where we turn, a stone pile is there to lead us on, or lead us astray. True markers or false, we have no way of telling. They all lead down.

We soon find ourselves scrambling along ledges that even an outlaw, hard-pressed, wouldn't attempt. "At least we have the satisfaction of pioneering a new route," I say.

"I hate it when we pioneer," Milzer says, lowering his pack down a short cliff.

Finally we reach the floor of a side canyon called the Beaver Box. Beaver dams block the streambed, trapping runoff in narrow pools cold to the touch. The temperature has dropped a few degrees since sunrise. Milzer zips up his parka. "If the sun gets any higher, I'll freeze to death."

A strip of willow and tamarisk borders the Dirty Devil at the mouth of the tributary. The river runs a greenish brown, sliding down the gorge. It drains the waterless deserts above, fingering back into the Blue, the Red, the Last Chance. An upper branch of the Dirty Devil reaches close to the uranium-riddled slopes of Temple Mountain, the source of the rock that turned Hiroshima into a desert of its own.

With some reluctance, we decide to wade down the river to a place I noticed earlier on the map. It's a box canyon called No Mans. Using driftwood sticks to probe for holes, we slosh through the muddy water, fed by spring runoff. Sand bars turn liquid with each step. The boundary between water and earth, river and sand disappears. Walking knee-deep, I hit a quicksand pocket and sink to the waist. It takes only a moment to extricate myself. Wet and cold, we continue following the river's course, pushing against an upstream wind.

A few stunted cottonwoods grow at the mouth of No Mans where we leave the river and head up the side canyon. Handholds, carved in the cliff, lead us into a cave where we find an old campsite. Charcoal and stone flakes litter the sandy floor. I recognize the nocked end of an arrow. Holding it up to the light, I check the shaft, still smooth and true. Nothing disappears completely. Sooner or later it all ends up in Shirley's rock shop.

Higher up the gorge we find a stone ramp and the remnants

of a horsetrail, leading out. This is unexpected since I'd heard the only way into this place is from the river. We follow the hidden trail to an upper bench and locate a way to the rim. Whoever named No Mans may have intended to mislead others into thinking it was inaccessible from the tablelands above, a place no man could reach. Fugitive country.

We walk the river again, returning against the current. On a terrace above the channel lies the skeleton of a horse, disarticulated and strewn about by coyotes. With a single skull among so many long bones, the animal might have had eight legs like Odin's legendary horse.

"We're dealing with a different mythology here," Milzer says. He picks up a femur, studies it with a slight cock of the head, and flings it up, letting the bone spin end over end. Strapping the skull to my pack, I continue up the Dirty Devil, bent like a medieval penitent. At the foot of the trail, I top a cairn with the skull to mark the true route.

Across from Robbers Roost Canyon we take shelter in Angel Cove, an immense scoop weathered out of the canyon wall. It has a good spring, screened by a scrub oak thicket. The cliffs bulge around us. "Like rolls of fat," Milzer says. "Look over there— double chins, a pot belly, and other miscellaneous, unidentified protuberances along the rim."

Evening winds pick up, spiraling within the alcove. They climb the Beauford scale until a gust hits camp with enough force to snuff out the stove flame. The two of us scramble around, piling rocks on our gear to keep things from blowing away. Milzer grabs the toilet paper just as it becomes airborne. He weighs it down with a pack, muttering something about "dharma bum wad."

We settle in for the night where the Wild Bunch once took refuge. Stories about the gang still circulate among the cattlemen in southern Utah, the region where Butch Cassidy was born. One of them, rancher Wallace Ott, told me he met Butch Cassidy in the late 1930s, years after the newspapers had reported the outlaw's death.

"It was in the spring," Wallace began, wearing a snap-button shirt and cowboy boots, "My neighbor Lige Moore came over one morning and asked me if I wanted to see Butch Cassidy.

That was the name he fixed up for himself. His real name was LeRoy Parker.

"'Well, Butch Cassidy is dead isn't he?' I told Lige.

"'That's what most everybody thinks,' Lige said, 'but he's over to my place now if you'd like to see him.'"

Lige Moore was a Texan, an expert with the six shooter who always wore a ten-gallon hat. He had met Cassidy on a cattle drive years before.

Rumors that Cassidy survived a shootout with soldiers in South America have persisted over the years. While historians have tried to sort out the evidence, and the lack of it, the legend has taken on a life of its own. During his career as an outlaw, Cassidy turned escape into an art form. He eluded his pursuers by outriding them on the trail and then by obscuring his identity when he went into hiding. He changed his name and gait, his habits and tastes — all to throw off the detectives who never stopped hunting him. At times he tried to give up his outlaw ways but without success. His past kept returning to haunt him.

"We talked most all morning," Wallace continued. "Butch said he was raised in such poor condition down here to Circleville, he ended up stealing from the rich and giving to the poor.

"After things got too warm for him here, he then went to South America and for a long while lived peacefully. But his past caught up with him. He came back to the United States and went to California first. Then he helped ol' Pancho Villa in Mexico. They was having a big revolution there and Pancho Villa paid him some real good money. He returned and lived a peaceable life."

The man who called himself Butch Cassidy told Wallace Ott that in the end he staged his own death. His last escape was from himself. "There's no question about it," Wallace adds, "that was Butch Cassidy I talked to."

As I stood up to go, I noticed a plaque on the wall of the rancher's home: "Trust Everyone But Brand Your Cattle."

Under the arching rock of Angel Cove, I fall asleep listening to the wind. It moves through the trees, moaning like an angel tangled in the branches.

Roadman

Back on the rim the next day, we head toward the southeastern corner of Utah, driving for an hour without passing another vehicle. The highway skirts the upper end of Lake Powell, gaining elevation as it threads between the Black Hole of White Canyon and the Tables of the Sun. Reaching Cedar Mesa, the road levels off. Only a handful of park rangers at Natural Bridges National Monument live year-round on this remote, 500-square-mile plateau. Incised by deep canyons, the surface lies cracked open to the sky.

We pull off at the head of Grand Gulch to check the old Mormon wagon road and sink to our ankles in mud. Milzer suggests I consider getting a four-wheel-drive truck. But a standard truck with enough clearance, I argue, can take you most places you need to go. If it gets too rough, you simply park the truck and walk. And being more vulnerable to weather, you become more aware of it. The two of us clomp back through the mud, more aware than ever of needing to veer south into Arizona and New Mexico to find drier weather.

Our road skirts a pair of high buttes known as the Bears Ears and angles down the east side of Cedar Mesa. Rain overtakes us at Comb Ridge, an 800-foot-high escarpment running eighty miles into Arizona, and an hour later it suddenly stops. The pavement switches instantly from wet to dry as we breach the rain cell and enter a duststorm south of White Mesa. Moving sand hugs the ground as wind churns the dust-clogged air, turning the sky yellow.

The highway descends the cliffs above Bluff and turns to follow the San Juan River, making a wide bend through town. A few stores and gas stations line the main road the way trees crowd a river bank. Less than 300 people live here, many in pioneer houses altered over the years to make room for growing families. We cut through a gridwork of back streets, passing the old county jail. Carved on the stone wall is a reminder, "Obedience to the Law Means Freedom."

Mormon settlers founded Bluff in 1880 when the Hole-in-the-Rock Expedition ground to a halt from sheer exhaustion. In an epic journey, the wagon train took six months to cross the canyon lands from Escalante. They had expected to cover the distance in six weeks.

"It is the roughest country you or anybody else ever seen," wrote pioneer Elizabeth Decker. "It's nothing in the world but rocks and holes, hills and hollows. The mountains are just one solid rock as smooth as an apple."

Members of the expedition had less than twenty miles to go before reaching their goal at Montezuma Creek. But unable to push any farther, they lost momentum. The expedition stopped at the first spot on the San Juan River wide enough to plant crops and lay out a townsite.

Dry brush clings to the edge of the highway outside town where runoff from the pavement provides just enough moisture to sustain life. At this time of year, the scant vegetation has grown brittle, taking on the color of sandstone. Like roadside plants, the desert draws us closer to water. The cold season has its smoke-gray clouds and black pools; the wet season has its blood-red flash floods; the dry season has its waterpockets evaporating into thick green broth and its virga sweeping the high desert with blue wisps of dry rain.

The duststorm eases by the time we enter the redbeds near the Valley of the Gods. Mexican Hat lies a few miles ahead. The town takes its name from a giant sombrero-shaped rock balanced on a neck of sandstone. On April Fool's Day the local paper printed a doctored photo showing an empty pedestal with a pile of rubble at its base. Taken in by the prank, some of the townspeople drove out to look at the remnants of their landmark.

Gold drew prospectors to Mexican Hat in the 1890s, and oil brought the wildcatters in 1908. A few pumps still operate on the edge of town whenever the price of oil climbs high enough to show a profit. Gas stations and a couple of motels cater to sightseers and river runners in season. Where the highway curves down to the bridge spanning the San Juan, we stop at a cafe and order bowls of mutton stew. Across the bridge lies the Navajo reservation. A pair of Indian cowboys chalk up pool cues on the bar side of the room. Old saddles hang on the walls next to cow skulls and a beer can collection.

Below us, the river sweeps toward a gorge where rock layers angle upward into walls hundreds of feet high. The San Juan enters the canyon, looping back and forth in a series of horseshoe bends called the Goosenecks. Floating through twenty-three miles of these entrenched meanders gains only seven straight-line miles on the map. Geologists believe the course of an ancestral river determined the canyon's topography. It once snaked across a level floodplain lying above the present rim. As the surrounding land uplifted, the river cut deeper without straightening the kinks.

Four sacred rivers border the Navajo homeland: the Rio Grande, the Little Colorado, the Colorado, and the San Juan. In the past whenever the Navajo people crossed one of these, they prayed and left a pinch of pollen or a piece of turquoise on the bank. Out of respect, they refrained from tossing the offering directly in the water. Instead, they placed it close enough to the river for the lapping water to carry it away.

Maps once labeled the gorge of the San Juan as an "Impassable Cañon," and an accurate survey of the river wasn't made until the 1920s. During the mapping, the surveyors heard an Indian call it "mad water." With a twisting course and sand waves that appear without warning, the name fits. And before a dam was built upstream, the flow was unpredictable. Every season the San Juan flooded; every few decades it dried up.

During one drought, a prospector panned a small fortune in gold dust from a sandbar downstream. But the river soon rose and reclaimed his bonanza. Too much water can be as much a problem in the desert as too little. He waited twenty years without luck for the low water to return. In despair, he walked onto the bridge one night and jumped, disappearing in the swirling current below. A few years later, the river again dropped low.

On an earlier trip to the San Juan, I drove across the reservation at night. My headlights picked out a Navajo standing on the shoulder with his hands in his pockets. He needed a ride. A Navajo often won't stick out his thumb when hitchhiking. The traditionals believe a person raised properly will give what is needed without being asked. I pulled over, opening the door on the passenger side.

A man wearing an army field jacket climbed in awkwardly, his movements thickened by heavy drinking. I told him I was going as far as Mexican Hat. Speaking slowly, dredging his memory for words, he said he wanted to go with me.

As we crossed Monument Valley, my passenger sat motionless, staring blankly ahead. Before us, a line of pinnacles stood against the night sky in dark iconic profile. After a few miles, the Navajo spoke in a voice much clearer than before. "I'm a Roadman," he said.

A Roadman is a priest of the Native American Church, known for the use of peyote as a sacrament, and also known for its prohibition against drinking. I took my eyes off the road and glanced at him. He was younger than I first thought, in his late twenties, with straight black hair hanging loose to his shoulders.

"You thought we didn't drink," he said. "Maybe some of us do." He laughed and said something in Navajo. All I caught were the words for whiskey, *toh lizhin,* meaning "dark water."

"I was in Vietnam," he continued, "Long-range reconnaissance. Got shot in the leg. There's a metal rod from here all the way down here." He motioned from knee to ankle. "I used to be a runner, almost state champ. But I can't run now."

He turned to stare out the side window, silent. Then he said in a low voice, "My wife is ready to leave me."

Before I could respond, he began crying very softly. I tried to reassure him, saying something about how it was hard to stay balanced in this crazy world. Navajo believe healing comes about when holiness is restored, renewing a sense of balance and harmony.

As the road curved to the east, the Roadman turned toward me and asked, "Do you want to learn a Navajo prayer?"

Before I could answer, he added, "Yes, it's a good prayer. I'll teach it to you."

He sat up straight and began to chant in Navajo with a voice deep and formal. His right hand moved before him in a series of strong ritual gestures. "It's very simple," he said when he finished. "You can learn it."

Beginning the prayer again, the Roadman held his hand before him. He moved it downward, without hesitation, and said in English, "Mother in the earth." And he brought his hand up before his face. "Father in the sky." And he gestured forward and backward. "From where the sun rises. To where the sun sets."

He motioned to the right and to the left. "To the south and to the north." And brought his hand to his chest. "All in my heart," he said. And again more softly, "All in my heart."

We crossed the bridge over the dark waters of the San Juan, running fast and broken below. Mad water. I pulled over on the far side. The Roadman had me repeat the prayer several times, making a few corrections. When I finally got it right, he opened the door and began walking off with a slight limp. "Use it any time you need it."

Done with the mutton stew, Milzer and I leave Mexican Hat and cross the bridge into the Navajo country. The road climbs steeply. Far to the south, I notice the stone pillars of Monument Valley. Having set the scene for so many western movies they now stand detached from their own surroundings, a John Ford backdrop floating in the dust haze. We turn off on a long backroad, crossing into Arizona and reaching the highway at Mexican Water. Passing a few miles south of the point where the four states meet, we cut across the northeast corner of Arizona and take our bearings from the snow-covered Chuska Mountains ahead. A layer of smoky clouds has settled at the foot of the range, severing the higher slopes from the redrock beneath.

As we drive, I tell Milzer about the last trip my brother and I made together. We flew back to Virginia for a funeral and late at night drove into Washington, D.C., to the Vietnam Veterans Memorial. Neither of us had seen it before. More than a dozen people wandered about searching for names engraved on the black slabs of stone. A sense of deep loss hung in the air. John hunted for the names of friends killed in action and for those he had never heard from again. He felt uneasy being at the wall and said, "I hope I don't find my own name here."

Farther east, we enter New Mexico. As the road climbs a slight rise, Ship Rock suddenly rears into view. The jagged monolith breaches the surface, rising more than 1,000 feet above the desert grasslands. This once-buried formation, the neck of an ancient volcano, surfaced when the surrounding land eroded away.

Two dogs wrestle in the main street as we enter the town of Shiprock, bringing us to a momentary halt. Enjoying the commotion, a Navajo waits behind the wheel of a pickup with a grin matching the curve of his hat brim. A sign across the street advertises "Rams and Billy Goats For Sale," and another outside the Chat and Chew cafe promises mutton stew and fry bread. A skim of dust covers puddles of standing water next to the road.

Again the San Juan River flows through a town, far upstream from Mexican Hat. We cross it, passing the "Kwalty" garage and a large revival tent pitched next to a double-wide. Several months earlier a Native American Church tipi stood in the same place. Some Navajo take the blood of Christ as their sacrament and some choose peyote. Others, the ones who call the land their church, continue to use corn pollen for their prayers.

Beyond a crested ridge called the Hogback, we leave the reservation and continue east toward Farmington. A driver, hunched over the steering wheel of a pickup, guns past the dregs of oil-and-gas development choking the strip of highway. Run-down houses line the road, and spare-time farms crowd the river banks. Inspired by the setting, Milzer works on the lyrics for a country-western song. "I think I'll call it, 'Excuse me while I apologize.'"

Encircled Mountain

Twin Angels rises to the east, a stark pinnacle on the rim of starker badlands. Scott Milzer and I catch sight of the landmark, a day after leaving the Dirty Devil.

Sagebrush plains break off at right angles on each side of the overlook where we stand, southeast of Farmington. Cliff and slope plunge into ravines banded in shades of white and washed purples. Wide spaces open to the north, stretching to the La Sal Mountains of Colorado, the sacred mountain of the north for the Navajo. South of us stands El Huerfano, a solitary mesa known as Dzil Na'oodilii, "the mountain around which traveling was done."

We have reached the Dinetah, the old Navajo homeland, a region lying outside the reservation and within a major oil-and-gas field. It is as close to a place of origin for them as we are likely to find. From here, the multiple trails leading deeper into the past grow fainter until there are no tracks left to follow. The Dinetah is where the stories of the Navajo people begin.

Needing to stretch our legs, Milzer and I sidestep below the rim. Recent storms across the Four Corners have saturated the claystones, leaving the surface slick underfoot and many of the backroads impassable. We planned to drive south to Chaco Canyon before swinging west to Burntwater, but the road is too muddy. We'll have to widen the arc.

On an earlier trip to the Dinetah, I joined anthropologist John Farella and two Navajo friends in Cañon Largo. As the aroma of fresh coffee drifted through camp, Cowboy Nez sat up in the back of a pickup where he had been sleeping under a tarp. A drenching rain had come during the night, carried by gusts of wind. The old Navajo didn't speak much English, but he knew what he wanted. "Coffee!" he demanded. "I want coffee."

Cowboy Nez, in his mid-eighties, and his son Ben had joined Farella to explore a string of ruined pueblitos scattered among 400-foot-deep canyons. The Navajo people, joined by Pueblo refugees, had built these fortified villages in the early eighteenth century. The idea of Navajos settling into stone pueblos didn't fit the standard image of nomadic herdsmen.

The ambiguity of the Dinetah attracted Farella. He sensed the real story had slipped between the cracks. The evidence didn't fit into the neat categories where the archeologists had sorted it. He had come here to look at sites dating from a pivotal moment in Navajo history, a period when Blessingway emerged as the core ceremony and the integrating force in their way of life.

"Blessingway," Farella told me, "is the ritual enactment of hózhó. It's often translated as beauty and harmony, but there's a lot more to it. Even some Navajos spend their lives trying to understand it." The anthropologist walked about with his boot laces untied, gathering up his gear. A stubble on his chin was the first sign of the winter beard he often let grow.

"The Blessingway ritual doesn't create predictability," he added, tossing a bedroll in the back of the pickup. "It doesn't let you avoid failure. That's part of living. What it does is let you walk through it. It gives you something to fall back on."

The story of Changing Woman forms the core of Blessingway, a ceremony meant to restore holiness and beauty to lives grown disordered. As the one who created human life and sustains it, she represents the animating force of nature. The Dinetah is her place of origin.

When First Man and First Woman lived at Huerfano, a dark raincloud settled upon Ch'oolii, a butte to the east now known as Gobernador Knob. First Man went to investigate, singing Blessingway songs as he walked. Once on the summit, he heard the cry of a baby and began to search for it in the mist. Moving closer he found Changing Woman lying in a cradleboard made of rainbows, laced with zigzag lightning. First Man picked up the foundling, recognizing Darkness as her mother and Dawn as her father.

Navajo petroglyphs of *ye'ii,* the Holy People, covered cliffs near camp. Much of the rock art resembled the stylized sand paintings still used by traditional healers. For unknown reasons, most medicine men stopped depicting the Holy People in permanent form when the Navajo left this region in the eighteenth century. Now, after a singer has portrayed the sacred figures in a dry painting, he destroys the image and scatters the pigments.

Among the forms pecked into the rock were those representing the twin brothers, Monster Slayer and Born for Water. These sons of Changing Woman were charged with ridding the world of monsters. Some Navajo consider the chantway monsters to be alien gods. Others see them as a metaphor for forces diverting the flow of life into destructive channels, states such as fear, anger, depression, and illness. Over time, the twins destroyed many of the monsters but not all. Changing Woman told her sons to let cold, hunger, poverty, and old age remain, realizing they might be useful.

Everybody packed into Farella's pickup for the drive to a pueblito called Old Fort. Ben sat next to his father. In the 1930s, Cowboy Nez anticipated the stock reduction ordered by the federal government. He sold his herd before prices dropped and bought savings bonds, using them to put his children through college. Ben earned a master's degree and returned to the reservation to run a school for many years. Tiring of the job, he went home to live his version of a traditional lifestyle. Between trips to Europe for dance workshops, Ben spent his days herding sheep and reading works by the Zen masters.

"People tell me I herd the sheep too much," he said. "But it turns the inside out and lets me look clearly at myself. It makes everything simple."

An hour later we reached the rim of a canyon. High on a ridge to the east stood Gobernador Knob, where First Man found Changing Woman long ago. The old man climbed stiffly from the pickup carrying a sport coat in case of rain. With a smile on his face, he hobbled down the hill to the ruins crowding the end of a promontory.

Sheer cliffs protected the site on three sides, while a high stone wall, built without a gateway, guarded it on the mesa side. The original occupants must have entered the compound by ladder. Navajo Indians, joined by Pueblo refugees fleeing Spanish rule, had constructed strongholds throughout the region. They lived during a dangerous time, reflected in the defensive layout of the village.

We passed through a collapsed section of the perimeter wall into a plaza flanked by crumbling roomblocks. Fragmentary walls rose from mounds of stone rubble. The pueblo was different from others I had seen. Remains of a forked-stick hogan stood next to ruined masonry dwellings. The architectural mix resembled the pragmatic homesteads still found on the reservation. On my way to the Dinetah, I'd passed Navajo camps where a traditional hogan sat next to a cinderblock house and a mobile home.

The old Navajo had been wandering alone among the ruins, carefully examining the site. This was new to him. He thought the Navajo people had always lived in hogans built of wood and mud, never square-cornered houses built of stone. Ben thought the forked-stick structure indicated a ritual-teaching area and the surrounding rooms had served as living quarters. As he talked, the Navajo sheepherder took off his shirt and tied it around his head, turban-style.

"This is strange," Ben said, pausing among the collapsed walls, growing uncomfortable in the close quarters of the compound. He found it hard to believe Navajos would choose to settle in such confined places. But when his ancestors lived here, mounted Ute Indians, armed with Spanish muskets, had swept through the region hunting slaves. "I guess if people are trying to kill you," he said, "you'll do anything."

Harried by their enemies, the Navajo drifted away from the Dinetah. To remain free they gave up living in stone villages and scattered. They cast off Pueblo ways and shifted their energies to herding and raiding, returning to their fields when necessary for planting and harvesting. They kept on the move, making it difficult for slave hunters, missionaries, and tax collectors to find them. At this moment in time, Blessingway emerged as the central rite of the Navajo, a way to restore order to a way of life grown chaotic.

After abandonment, a stillness settled over these canyons. Yesterday, Cowboy Nez noticed the quiet. He turned to his son saying, "It's as if the world said, 'Just listen.' "

At daybreak I got up and started fixing breakfast. The air hung still and heavy with moisture after a night rain. Poking the wet ashes of the campfire, I looked across the canyon floor where a natural-gas-well pad stood, dull-gray and black. The valves, pipes, and sheet-metal tank sat detached from the surrounding cliffs as if the machinery had dropped from the sky. Disconnected from the surface world, it tapped into unseen sources of energy within the deeper geologic strata.

The contrast of metal and sandstone reminded me of something I couldn't quite place. I filled the coffee pot and threw in some grounds, waiting for the memory to surface. All at once the story came back as clearly as when I first heard it. This was the place my brother described; this was where it happened.

The story he told began when he left his home at the Grand Canyon, driving a gray jeep called the Colonel Mosby. He was with a group of friends traveling in a caravan of six trucks. They kept to the backroads for two weeks across the Four Corners country. I have an old photograph of him taken at that time. He sits on a rock ledge wearing a felt hat, mountain-creased, a silver bowguard on his wrist, and a pistol strapped to his side.

As they entered the northwestern corner of New Mexico, one of the trucks broke down. The others headed to the nearest town for repairs, while John and one friend of his turned their trucks up a broad wash. Without knowing it, my brother had found his way into the heart of the Dinetah. At the time, he didn't know its significance or even his precise location. All he knew was the place had a beauty to it that drew him in.

John and his friend drove their trucks along a well-graded road that kept to the floor of Cañon Largo, avoiding the sandy wash. The farther up the drainage they drove, the prettier it became. The canyon narrowed protectively, balanced with the right proportion of rock and sky and tree. But the more beautiful the canyon became, the angrier John grew. Pipelines crisscrossed the terrain; pumps cluttered the canyons and mesatops. A grid of oil- and gas-well pads and access roads overlaid the natural setting.

The two friends turned off the main road into a fine side canyon, hoping to find a place to camp. But around the first bend they found it marred by another well pad and another storage tank. John had seen enough. "Your brother just lost it," his friend later told me.

They stopped their trucks and got out. It was getting dark as John put on a pair of moccasins to obscure his tracks. After inspecting the natural-gas tank and opening a few valves, he returned to his jeep and reached behind the seat. And pulled out a deer rifle. His friend, who had fought as a door gunner in Vietnam, grabbed another weapon.

"Watch this," John told him.

He took aim and squeezed the trigger. The storage tank exploded. Monster Slayer stirred once more. Moving quickly, they jumped in their trucks and sped up-canyon. Not knowing where to run, the pilot and the gunner drove blindly for a number of miles before pulling far off the roadway. They hadn't planned an escape route. It was a spontaneous act, unrehearsed and without thought for the consequences.

By now it was full dark. They had passed a security truck earlier in the day and knew the sheriff would have a description of their vehicles. They hid their jeeps in a stand of piñon trees. Walking back to the road, they brushed out their tracks. That night the two of them watched a glow in the sky to the north as the fire burned.

Things might have been different if I had been there, maybe not. Sometimes I checked my brother's impulses, but at times he drew me into situations I wouldn't have chosen on my own.

The next day the fugitives laid low, hiding in a cave overlooking the canyon. They spent the day watching as a search party combed the area. Trucks prowled the main road, hunting for any sign of them. At one point a helicopter passed overhead, flying a search pattern, but they were too well-hidden. The chopper kept flying south and didn't return. When darkness came the second night, John and his friend left the Dinetah and drove without stopping to their homes at the Grand Canyon.

My brother never said much about the incident. On his return, he gave me a terse account of what happened without trying to justify his actions. It wasn't meant as a protest, he said. What occurred was a private act, as much a prayer as a political statement. As far as he was concerned the incident was finished, buried in the past. He never mentioned it again.

Milzer and I climb back to the overlook at Twin Angels, passing the stiff hide of a coyote among the broken beer bottles. Snow lies plastered against a prominent knoll nearby, topped by the remnants of a prehistoric shrine.

An ancient roadway, running almost true north from the ceremonial center at Chaco Canyon, reaches this point and disappears. Archaeologists call it the Great North Road. In the eleventh century, Anasazi Indians constructed an extensive system of roads that followed bearings so straight they cut notches through the hills instead of going around them. They were paved and curbed, had a standard width, and were flanked by roadside shrines. Pointing north, this roadway had all the features of a well-engineered road except for one. It lacked a destination. The Chaco road ran straight for more than thirty miles until breaking off where the land falls away to the north.

Many Pueblo Indians locate the opening to the Underworld somewhere to the north. Traditionally, this opening serves as the place of emergence and the entrance to the Home of the Dead. Although the specific location shifts with different variations of the story, the direction holds. The Great North Road heads north, ending nowhere in particular.

Archaeologists have attempted to decipher the cosmology of the ancient Chacoans, drawing on concepts of sacred geography expressed by modern Pueblo Indians. But sometimes we take these ideas too literally. A clan history often describes how the people found where they were meant to settle only after a long migration in search of the Middle Place, the center of the universe. But the Middle Place can also lie in the plaza of the pueblo farther down the river and in the next one beyond it. We imagine the holy lands as a fixed location, staked to a particular piece of ground, when all we have is holiness and a place to recognize it.

Another storm is moving in from the west. If we aim directly for Burntwater, we'll collide head-on with it. By heading east we might stay in front of the weather for a day or two. Letting the storm push us deeper into New Mexico, we leave Twin Angels and drive toward the ruins of Bandelier.

A few miles down the road we stop at the Blanco Trading Post. Notices taped next to the entrance advertise fat sheep for sale and a Pentecostal revival. Inside, a wood-burning stove heats a room filled with saddles and skeins of wool, old pawn and junk food. A Navajo, standing stiff and formal in his black hat and turquoise necklace, trades at the counter. As his grandchildren check out the videos for rent, we carry cups of road coffee back to the truck. A car parked in front has a license plate with the New Mexico state motto, "Land of Enchantment." We'll see, soon enough.

Brothers of Light

As we cross the Continental Divide, the pattern of erosion shifts. Dry washes reverse direction, fingering eastward through a land shaped by a different past. Adobe homes replace hogans; strings of red chiles hang next to doors painted turquoise blue.

"Western Gothic," Scott Milzer says, eyeing a bleached cow skull on a gate post. Behind it, rains have splattered mud against the foot of a wall, staining the adobe red. "This is the land of lizard-skin boots and elk-antler chairs."

We pass through the frame and enter a Georgia O'Keefe landscape. Ahead stands a line of red cliffs against a paint-blue sky. Below it lies the Ghost Ranch where the artist lived for many years.

Weather reports keep warning of another big storm moving in from the west. To stay ahead of the system, I turn toward the Rio Grande. Layer by layer, the road cuts through the mesalands deeper than an archaelogical trench, uncovering the older configurations. As we descend, the valley widens to catch the full light of day.

The road leads past Chili to Hernandez through a rural sprawl of new trucks, old trailers, and scaled-back dreams. The surroundings appear vaguely familiar, and a moment later I make the connection. This is where Ansel Adams took one of his best-known photographs — "Moonrise, Hernandez, New Mexico."

Driving south at sunset fifty years ago, the legendary photographer noticed the moonlight edging the gravestones next to the old village. Adams had an eye for light and knew he was losing it. He pulled off the road with only enough time for one shot, a single instant. His camera sliced across the field of view, exposing a black-and-white image of adobe, mountain, and sky. In it, a line of blank walls stretches beneath the Sangre de Cristo range with a lens of clouds floating above the mountains, forming a higher, luminous range. And above it glows the moon, suspended at the moment before true dark.

Hernandez has aged, grown more complex over the years. New layers have accumulated on top of the old. A highway maintenance shed partially screens the adobe church from view. Metal has reshaped its roofline, and a chain-link fence encloses the cemetery. But beyond the village, the mountains and the vast sky still wait for another moonrise.

Traffic thickens on the way into Espanola. The flow of cars and pickups slows where the quick-stop, pump-your-own, drive-through architecture crowds the roadside. Just beyond the Saints and Sinners Bar I spot a lone pilgrim, a reminder this is Holy Week. With a wooden cross over his shoulder, the *peregrino* strides toward a shrine lying miles away in the foothills of the Sangre range. He walks with a yellow T-shirt tied around his head, beneath a sky washed yellow by a sudden fall of afternoon light.

Each year thousands of pilgrims converge on an old adobe chapel in the village of Chimayo. New Mexicans have been making the annual pilgrimage to the shrine of El Santuario for two centuries.

On my first trip to Chimayo, I found discarded crutches covering the walls of a chapel where a girl prayed to a saint dressed in doll clothes and costume jewelry. Nearby, the faithful lined up to gather handfuls of dirt, thought to perform miraculous cures, from a hole in the floor of the shrine. Some rubbed afflicted parts of their bodies with the healing earth; others took a handful home to mix with their food. Lawyers and artists from Santa

Fe, the cultural center of the Southwest, reached into the hole as deeply as the rest.

What for them was normal and proper, struck me as strange. I had entered a region where the voice of suffering and redemption still resonated. But instead of simply turning away, I decided to see where it might lead. The annual pilgrimage would take place in two weeks. I decided to return and walk with them.

At two in the morning, the beginning of April, I parked the truck at a shopping mall on the outskirts of Santa Fe. Locals had warned me not to leave it along the road; the tires might be gone when I got back. I stepped out into the night as a coyote called in the distance. It was Good Friday. Snow blew directly from the north, head-on, putting me in a somber mood. The weather had taken a turn for the worse. Unsure of what lay ahead, I began walking to Chimayo, twenty-eight miles away.

No other pilgrim was in sight as I started up the steep grade north of Santa Fe, following the main highway. Even late at night, a few cars continued to fly along the slick surface. A few hours before, a car had struck and killed a pilgrim along this same stretch of road. Each approaching car became a startling encounter, quickly fading to dark silence.

To do the walk properly, I traveled light. I'd left behind my pack and cold-weather gear, carrying a pint of water in one jacket pocket and an orange in the other. I wore jeans and a baseball cap. This wasn't the way to dress for a long trek in a snowstorm, but then comfort wasn't the point. The customary way to reach Chimayo was to do it the hard way. Even moving at a quick pace, I soon began to shiver. A wind-blown layer of snow coated my front half.

Snow had filled the spaces between the trees. The hills looked steeper and colder than when I started, floating ghost-like against the pale-gray night. The wind blew stronger, forcing me to walk with head bent, watching tendrils of snow sweep the edge of the blacktop.

For a couple of hours I walked alone without seeing another pilgrim. My legs already ached from the hard pavement, and I wondered what I was doing here. Perhaps this dark night was part of every pilgrimage, but I felt misled. I suspected the other walkers had found rides back to town and were now curled up in their warm beds. Maybe I'd gotten the wrong date.

As I walked past a truck parked on the side of the road, a voice called out, asking if I wanted a cup of coffee. A man, sitting in the front seat of his pickup, said he had been up all night helping the peregrinos. He did this as his own penance. About 1,200 people had passed him since last midnight, he said, surprised I hadn't seen anybody.

I finished the coffee and continued down the empty road, walking mile after mile, doing nothing else. Waves of strength alternated with longer stretches of tiredness. During the hard times I got angry with myself. I'd walked farther on rough trails in a single day and felt much better than I did now. Because of all the miles I'd covered in the past, I thought I deserved an exemption from discomfort, a dispensation. It never came. I passed a hand-lettered sign placed next to the highway reading, "Shoe Repair," with an arrow pointing to a closed shop.

Miles passed until the sky lightened enough to expose a vague pattern of hills farther away. After a long night, daylight came unexpectedly, bringing with it the sharp scent of junipers. Clouds hung low; snowflakes drifted down aimlessly. Soon I caught a whiff of piñon smoke curling from an adobe house tucked among the trees.

Near the turnoff to Chimayo, a cowboy mounted his horse and rode through a gate. He reined toward the cloud-hidden slopes of the upper hills and soon disappeared. Earlier I had passed a couple of Indian pueblos. Another village spread somewhere off to the right, and Chimayo still lay ten miles ahead.

With daylight, peregrinos suddenly appeared on the road as if they had been here all along. They were now everywhere, crowding the shoulder and spilling onto the narrow highway in a staggered line. They surged uphill, a river that had reversed its course. Most were dressed in blacks and blues, matching the dull coats of primer on the low-riders coasting past.

The narrow road left behind the last houses and crossed several foothill spurs, radiating from the Sangre range. Arroyos undercut the roots of scrub trees, holding fast as the ground melted away beneath them. Crosses topped a few of the barren hills along the route. Two pilgrims passed me at a good clip carrying small crosses over their shoulders. Their faster pace reminded me of my own tiredness. My legs below the knees throbbed with a mixture of numbness and disembodied pain. Each step squeezed the blisters on my feet. I stopped thinking, since every thought drifted back to physical discomfort.

"It doesn't get any easier," a walker on his fourteenth pilgrimage told me. Ahead of him, two high school athletes in team jackets inched along, stiff with pain and walking bowlegged to ease the chafing. Thinking they were in good shape, they hadn't prepared for the undertaking. Many walkers purposely added to their suffering by not eating, drinking, or sitting down to rest until they reached their destination. Some fingered rosary beads as they went; one shouldered a heavy wooden cross.

The faithful of northern New Mexico had undertaken this pilgrimage for generations. And long before the Spanish, Pueblo Indians visited a shrine at the place they called Tsi Mayoh. After World War II, the popularity of El Santuario increased dramatically when survivors of the Bataan Death March returned to walk the pilgrim's road.

During the pilgrimage, an unspoken bond formed among the walkers. The peregrinos represented a cross-section of Hispanic society — the poor and the rich, the illiterate and the highly educated. Some talked about why they were walking; others kept it to themselves. By the end of the walk, the reasons no longer mattered

"There are many different reasons why people walk," said Viola Ortega, pausing for a brief rest. Although born and raised in Santa Fe, Viola was on her first pilgrimage. "Something very, very bad happened to me; I almost died. I vowed to God if I made it through I would make this walk."

She had come all the way from Santa Fe and was still going strong. Her companion, a veteran walker, had completed twenty-five pilgrimages. "You're enjoying yourself too much," he told her. "You're supposed to hurt."

When Viola asked about my work I told her I was a writer, but quickly added that I was walking in memory of my mother who had died a year ago, Good Friday. What I didn't tell her was I had chosen that reason for a cover story; it sounded more appropriate than saying I was here just to take notes. But my cover had taken on a life of its own. I thought of my mother often as I walked and remembered I'd been unable to cry over her death. Earlier as I traveled alone, surrounded by darkness and caught by a wave of tiredness, my eyes had filled with tears that didn't fall.

Topping the ridge above Chimayo, I looked into the narrow valley below. No wave of relief came with the first sight of the village, only the knowledge that it was still a mile away. And the last mile had thickened, compressing the distance, making each step an effort.

Passing the police barricades on the edge of town, I entered the narrow streets that threaded between old adobe houses. In the cold, snow-gray morning, with everyone on foot, with pilgrims huddled around warming fires, with the air itself charged with religious purpose, I found myself walking through a medieval town buried deep in America.

Reaching El Santuario, I stopped to rest among the graves lining the walkway to the little church. A grindstone, set at the base of a wooden cross, reminded visitors of the death that reduces all. Two pilgrims crawled past it, covering the last stretch on their knees. Under the blank sky, the warm tones of adobe had paled to gray. The corners of the church curved as smoothly as molded clay; the only sharp angles were the roofs covering the nave and bell towers. They seemed to be a later addition, perhaps the afterthought of a priest uncomfortable with the fleshy roundness of adobe.

A few Anglos wandered about, but not many, and even fewer tourists. They were easy to spot in their bright clothes and birdlike curiosity. To stop shivering, I got up and walked stiffly around the plaza. This didn't help so I returned to the church, the only place to get warm. Discarded staffs of those who had completed their pilgrimage leaned against the wall. I entered and took a seat in one of the pews toward the rear.

The mood of the walk settled over me. I had crossed into a world where suffering and death were faced with faith alone. I no longer saw the church and its worshipers the same way. The painted altar screen and carved *santos* no longer held any historical interest for me, and as works of art they were beside the point. I was too drained to think. If the wooden lips of a carved saint were to move, I'd answer politely. I was just another tired walker trying to get warm, thankful it was over.

Pilgrims filled the aisle, waiting their turns to enter the chapel and gather the *milagro* dirt. They slowly filed past a wooden railing worn smooth and yellowed by the hands of generations of worshipers. Above them hung a tortured Christ, carved and painted in the throes of agony. It was a reminder of those still walking.

For half the night I had walked, wondering about the purpose of this pilgrimage, hearing from others only elusive reasons. But the walk taught a lesson, drawing you outside yourself long enough to realize that without compassion, life dries up.

Leaving the church, I again crossed paths with Viola. Her daughters, who had come to drive her back to Santa Fe, offered me a lift. We loaded into the car and returned along the pilgrim's route.

A mile or two from the village, we passed a woman struggling up the hill under her own immense weight. Knowing how she suffered and the distance she had to cover, our hearts went out to her. "My God," Viola said as we drove by, "she'll never make it."

During Holy Week the following year, I returned to New Mexico. I planned to attend the ceremonies of a religious brotherhood known as the Penitentes, unsure of what I'd find.

Once in the foothills of the Sangre De Cristo mountains I began to catch whiffs of piñon smoke. The aroma, resinous and pungently sweet, brought back the mood of last year's pilgrimage. On the shoulder of the highway leading to the shrine walked knots of peregrinos. At Chimayo I stopped at the trading post next to the church to talk with Ray Bal, a dealer in saints and votive charms.

Ray looked surprised when I told him of my intention to visit Cordova for the Penitente services. His mother had grown up in that village. She had vivid memories of seeing blood streaming down the white pants of the Penitentes as they walked through the streets whipping themselves. Ray, who had lived here all of his life, asked if I had an invitation. I wasn't sure. Nothing formal, I told him. A local woodcarver had suggested I come for the ceremonies and mentioned, in passing, the possibility of a visit to the *morada,* a Penitente chapel.

"Be careful," Ray warned as I turned to leave. "You may be singled out, and who knows what will happen?"

Wondering if I'd misread the situation, I continued up the road to Cordova, thinking about the Penitentes. Called the Brothers of Light by some and known locally as Los Hermanos, they had traditionally practiced self-flagellation and other forms of extreme penance. They offered their suffering as an atonement for their sins and as a way to share the suffering of Jesus.

Both civil and religious authorities had persecuted the Penitentes over the centuries. But fifty years ago, the church recognized them as a legitimate order and the brotherhood agreed to undergo their penance in private. A local *santero,* a traditional carver, told me their rituals had died out, but I wasn't convinced. On the pilgrimage I learned how deeply the idea of suffering was ingrained in the character of this region.

Cordova lay in a deep fold of the Sangre range. From the ridge above it, I spotted a jumble of tin roofs marking the village. Stone fences divided the land into a patchwork of small fields and even smaller orchards. On the outskirts of town, a half-dozen pickups were parked at the cemetery. Bare mounds of earth covered several fresh graves decorated with bright plastic flowers. Several men sat next to an open grave, waiting patiently for another burial to begin.

Passing through the village, I followed narrow streets crowded between older adobe houses and a sprinkle of newer homes. The people have always built with materials readily available. Once it had been adobe, now it was cement block and corrugated metal.

Reaching the home of Sabinita Ortiz, the woodcarver I had spoken to earlier in the week, I knocked on the door. The *santera* had just returned from her pilgrimage to Chimayo and was surprised to see me. What I had taken to be an invitation, I now realized, had only been politeness. Her husband Cristobal joined us for a cup of coffee, and after some casual conversation, I asked Sabinita about the morada. She hesitated a moment before asking Cristobal if he would take me to it. Before we left, Sabinita reminded her husband to make sure he knocked on the chapel door before entering. She repeated her warning for emphasis.

"Take your truck," he told me as we stepped outside. "I may not want to stay as long as you're going to."

I followed him on a roundabout way that led to the back of a simple adobe building. Change comes slowly to Cordova, and the main road to the morada had never been widened for cars. The old Penitente chapel lay on the outskirts of town overlooking the upper valley of the Rio Quemado, the "burnt river." A thick-timbered cross stood above the chapel next to a row of graves. Across the valley the crest of the Sangre de Cristo mountains pushed into the clouds.

Several trucks were parked in the yard, and a number of men hovered near an outlying shed. They watched our approach with more curiosity than suspicion. Before we could knock on the morada door, out stepped a solid man in his early fifties, carrying himself with a leader's bearing. Cristobal introduced me to the Hermano Mayor, the Elder Brother of the Penitentes. Wearing a silver buckle inlaid with a turquoise bear paw, Joe Lopez had three faint cuts on his left cheek and his eyes appeared glassy from a lack of sleep and fasting. I had expected to meet someone hardened to pain and inured to the suffering of others. But the Elder Brother had a surprisingly gentle way about him. In a kind voice he invited me into the morada.

Cristobal abruptly announced he was leaving. "Stay as long as you want," he told me, hurrying to get back to his car. "It's okay."

Inside the morada, a few of the Penitente Brothers welcomed me with stiff formality. I followed them past a dark alcove in the rear of the room, catching a glimpse of a man lying on an adobe bench, unmoving. In sharp contrast, sunlight flooded through the windows of the front chapel onto whitewashed walls. As the Penitentes steered me to the altar I heard the deep, utter moan of someone in pain. The sound of human suffering caught me by surprise. It must have been the man lying in the back.

The Brothers hesitated and looked at me uneasily. After generations of persecution, they were unsure of my reaction. I acted as if nothing unusual had happened, and two of them went back to quiet the suffering man. The other Brothers led me across a plank floor into the chancel where they proudly introduced me to their saints.

Three powerful carvings by the nineteenth-century santero, Jose Rafael Aragon, stood before the altar. These museum-quality pieces were displayed shoulder-to-shoulder with gaudy plaster statues. Light-blue robes clothed the wooden saints, leaving their bleeding heads and hands uncovered. They appeared so real, the moan I heard could have come from any of them.

While I studied the carvings, a woman and her two children arrived and offered two votive candles to the Hermano Mayor. She knelt in prayer at the back of the chapel as the Brothers gathered to sing a hymn for the soul of the dead. I took a seat on an adobe bench near a woodburning stove. Their archaic song filled the small room, and without a church of my own I found myself praying in this Penitente morada for both the dead and the living.

After the hymn, the leader led me to the door. He mentioned they would walk throughout the night on *visitas* to various locations in the valley. When I asked him if these rounds were a time for doing penance, he answered evasively. "It is a time of prayer and meditation."

He invited me to come to the village church that night for Las Tinieblas, the earthquake ceremony. This was a Penitente observance, conducted without the presence of a priest, meant to evoke Christ's death on the cross, the moment when the earth shook, when darkness descended, when the graves opened. "Come early," the leader said, "but have patience. Don't be in a rush."

Driving back through town, I stopped to talk with Cristobal. He had asked me to check in with him before I left and seemed relieved that everything went well. Cordova, he thought, was the only remaining village where the Brothers still whipped themselves. They also carried crosses so heavy that men often collapsed beneath them. But it had been a few years, he said, since he had seen them drag chains through the streets.

Night had fallen by the time I returned to Cordova. The bell tower of the church served as a landmark to guide me through the unfamiliar alleys and unpaved streets. To reach the doors of the church, I crossed the *campo santo,* a small graveyard enclosed by a low wall. Once inside, the long interior was unexpectedly narrow since the thick adobe walls occupied so much space. High above, the Holy Spirit descended in the form of a bird painted on the whitewashed walls.

I noticed old Silvanita among the few villagers who had come early. Dressed in black, she sat in her pew as still as a rock, waiting for the ceremony to begin.

Last year I stopped to talk with her husband, the famous *santero* George Lopez. Silvanita greeted me at the front door with a babble of friendly Spanish. Almost ninety years old, she was bent with age to half my height. She turned and led me inside, gesturing toward the opposite wall. I was unprepared for what I saw. In the corner of their living room sat a death cart, and on it rode a skeleton carved from aspen wood, smooth and chalk white. It held a scythe. The old woman introduced me to the figure as casually as she would a relative. "La Muerte," she said in an eerily good-natured voice. "Death," she repeated.

After a long wait in the church I heard voices singing somewhere in the night beyond. The lights went out and the heavy wooden doors opened. The Brothers emerged from the pitch dark, lighting their way with kerosene lanterns. They filed across the graveyard singing a hymn in rough unison and passed into the church carrying crucifixes. As they walked through the nave, I noticed two hunched forms draped in black cloths, covering head and back. They shuffled down the aisle as slowly as wounded animals.

The Penitente Brothers sang another hymn before the altar and left by the side door of the sacristy. Their voices faded in the distance as somewhere in the dark church a young woman began to cry. When the lights came on, a couple of boys darted back to the main doors. I followed them to see what was happening. We crossed the graveyard and looked over the wall. The procession came down a side street and stopped. The black coverings were pulled off the humped forms, exposing the bare backs of two boys. The young Penitentes stayed bent over as others placed a heavy-timbered cross, longer than a man, on each back. The initiates staggered off barefoot, carrying their burdens into the night.

After a long interval, the main ceremony began. Strong voices, joined in song, approached the church. Soon a procession of about two dozen Penitente Brothers entered through the main doors. All were dressed in black with the Hermano Mayor leading from the rear. Their chant evoked darker ages, medieval nights. By now the church had filled with mothers and children who sang along with the Brothers. Crowding into the chancel, the Penitentes knelt to pray the rosary. The air was charged with expectation.

A row of candles burned on the altar above them; the rest of the church lay in darkness. The Penitente Brothers began singing a long hymn. At the end of each verse, a Brother pinched out the flame of another candle. The church grew steadily darker. When the light of the last flame died, the church fell into total darkness. All was eerily quiet in the moment signifying Christ's death. Suddenly a voice shouted out, and a terrific noise erupted, crashing in from all directions. Everyone was yelling, clapping, and stamping their feet. Unseen in the dark, the Brothers whirled ratchets and swung wooden rattles. A moan wove through the din as a wave of emotion flooded the church.

After the clamor tapered off to silence, a single voice in the dark uttered a prayer for the soul of a dead relative. Another voice did the same and then another prayed in turn as the waxy scent of extinguished candles hung in the air. After four or five prayers had been offered, the voice in the dark again called out. Again pandemonium broke loose.

Then without warning, after the noise had faded once more, all the lights flashed on. It happened quicker than the eye could adjust. There was a moment of blinding white before colors bled back into the field of vision. As the Brothers lined up facing the altar, the Hermano Mayor leaned over to a little girl sitting on her mother's lap. "Were you afraid?" he asked in a kind voice. She was too scared to answer and held tightly to her mother.

The Penitente brothers began singing Christ's farewell to the world as they left the church, walking backwards. Outside in the graveyard they lined each side of the walkway and continued singing as the villagers filed out. Starting low, the song lifted into the higher reaches before settling back to a middle, human range. The Brothers sang with one voice, filled with hope and strength.

Their song stayed with me as I drove back to Santa Fe. It was so distinct I thought I'd never forget it. But soon the tune I remembered wasn't the one they had sung. Memory had already worked it into something different from it was, diluting the force it held. By the time I reached town I'd lost it altogether, leaving the song far behind.

Stone Lions

L ayers of dried mud coat my boots. I glance at them and back at the road leading to Bandelier, and then down at the floor, caked with mud. A crust from Davis Gulch lies under one from the Dirty Devil and another from the Great North Road, each a distinct shade of weathered rock.

With a cliff wall on one side and a drop-off on the other, the highway grabs my full attention as it cuts up the face of a mesa. On impulse, Scott Milzer and I pass the turnoff to the ruins and continue on the road to Los Alamos.

After entering the mesatop city, we spend most of our time searching for a way back out. Home of a secret weapons laboratory, Los Alamos tries hard to be normal. Only an occasional restricted zone breaks the quiet regularity of house and yard. We pass streets named with a touch of pride after the nuclear test sites of Trinity and Bikini. Growing more disoriented by the layout of the town, I pull into a science museum to get directions.

Exhibits on nuclear weapons and missiles, lasers and supercomputers draw us in. We push buttons and read the spare commentary.

"I feel like an Anasazi walking through here," Milzer says. He hits another button as red lights flash. "This new technology fills me with enthusiasm and weariness. I can't keep up with it."

Working our way to the back corner, we find duplicates of

the world's first atomic bombs on display. The weapons have a clunky, boilerplate appearance, something Flash Gordon might have designed. One is labeled "Little Boy" and the other "Fat Man." Nothing sinister. Only cartoon names and metal casings are left to remind us of a pivotal event of the twentieth century.

During World War II, atomic scientists came to this remote mesa, determined to build a bomb before the enemy could do the same. The director of the nuclear weapons program was J. Robert Oppenheimer. Whenever possible, the scientist pulled on his cowboy boots and headed into the mountains on horseback.

Once a thunderstorm caught him on a ridge at midnight. Lightning began to strike. He continued riding through the storm until he came to a fork in the trail. If he took the direct way, he would soon be safely home. The other branch was longer but more beautiful. With lightning zigzagging across the night sky, he turned down the farther trail. His two loves, the desert and physics, came together at Los Alamos.

July, 1945, found Oppenheimer farther south in New Mexico, waiting deep in the Jornada del Muerto for the first detonation of an atomic bomb. He had chosen the name "Trinity" for the test site after reading the sonnets of John Donne. The poet's "three-personed God," with the power to break, blow, burn and to make new, caught his attention. The scientist was gambling that the horror of annihilation would bring peace to the world.

Five miles from ground zero at the forward bunker, Oppenheimer waited for the detonation. His final duty, as he saw it, was to bear witness. At the test site, scientists were taking side bets on the magnitude of the explosion; some thought it would trigger a chain reaction igniting the atmosphere. No one knew with any certainty what would happen.

After all the frantic months of experiment and calculation, the complex mathematics were reduced to a simple series of numbers: five . . . four . . . three . . . two . . . one. And then came a moment of terrifying beauty as the night sky split open with a light never seen before.

"What was that?" asked a blind woman riding with her sister on a distant highway. In an instant, the flash had penetrated her own darkness. The initial blast lasted nine seconds. A wave of searing heat struck the observers as a thundering roar echoed off the mountains and rolled across the desert, shaking an adobe house far away. The rancher looked outside and shouted to his wife, "The sun's rising in the wrong direction."

Later Oppenheimer described the reaction of the scientists at Trinity. "We knew the world would not be the same," he said, "A few people laughed. A few people cried. Most people were silent," he paused with tears in his eyes. "I remembered the line from the Hindu scripture, the *Bhagavad Ghita:* 'Now I am become Death, the destroyer of worlds.' I supposed we all thought that, one way or another."

At Trinity we crossed a threshold, entering a world where the dead could no longer be counted, where numbers gave way to sheer mass, where death became nameless. Leaving the museum, I pass an ash-white statue of the scientist wearing his porkpie hat and standing as still as a pillar of salt. It's a strange monument for a man of such restless energy, a man who was sustained in his work by what he called "the strange and compelling harmony of nature."

Returning to the truck, I notice splashes of dried mud on the truck fenders that match the colors on my boots. Strata accumulate. We carry with us traces of the past whether we intend to or not. Milzer and I leave the atomic city and intersect the road to Bandelier. It's late afternoon with clouds surging above the Jemez Mountains to the west. The park headquarters lies deep in Cañon de los Frijoles among the ruins of an Anasazi settlement. At the visitor center, a park ranger issues us a backcountry permit but warns that we might get snowed in.

After quickly throwing gear into our backpacks, we find the trailhead and begin walking toward the Shrine of the Stone Lions, six miles away. A friend told me if I ever had the chance to see the shrine, take it. To get there, Milzer and I will have to cross a high mesa sliced by gorges into *portreos*, flat-topped ridges fingering down from the mountains. Even pushing hard, we won't make it to the shrine before dark.

These mountain lions, carved from bedrock, date to prehistoric times. But Indians from nearby villages still visit the open-air site to pray and leave offerings. Men from Cochiti Pueblo paint the eyes and claws of the mountain lions with red ocher and inhale their breath before a hunt. Some Zuni Indians, living 200 miles to the south, travel to the shrine at the close of their Shalako dance. During this all-night ceremony, towering kachinas return to Zuni Pueblo to bless the people.

Often the Zuni leaders close Shalako to outsiders. So one December when a friend told me they planned to open it for the first time in several years, I went. Entering the pueblo, I found a few Indians standing around a warming fire. They were speaking Zuni among themselves, a language unrelated to any other. When I asked where I could find the ceremony, they politely directed me through the old village and past the mission church.

About a hundred spectators, mostly Anglo, waited in the cold. The crowd faced south, expecting the kachinas to appear across the dry bed of the Zuni River. Pale reds tinted a bank of altocumulus to the west. As I watched, the last light dropped from the clouds, and the whole sky brightened with an intense afterglow.

An old friend, backcountry guide Terry Gustafson, walked up with a wool hat pulled low over his ears. I had been expecting him. As we waited, a van cruised by with a teddy bear and a prayer feather dangling from the rearview mirror.

Finally, a tribal police car eased to a stop on the far side of the river with its lights flashing. Six Shalako, one for each kiva, filed into sight and lined up on the opposite bank. Someone turned off the revolving lights, and darkness settled over the village. Light from the sun, lying below the horizon, edged the rim of a new moon hanging just above it.

Shalako coincides with the approach of the winter solstice, the center point of the solar cycle. It also marks a return of the Zuni dead to the village, the Middle Place of the people. The event occurs where the center of time passes through the center of space. Each year, the kachinas enter the pueblo, renewing the story of a lost traveler who returns after being transformed into a spirit being.

The kachinas, standing ten feet tall, waited until full dark before crossing the footbridge. The sound of singing, accompanied by a rhythmic tinkling of seashells and turquoise, floated over to where we stood watch. Once across the river, the Shalako kachinas again stopped. No one knew how long they would wait before entering the village.

During the pause, Terry and I ducked into a Zuni home for a cup of coffee. A couple of kids sat in front of a satellite TV watching a boxer hammer away on his opponent. A large painting of the Zuni gods hung on one wall; family photos and sports trophies filled the others. Most of the relatives sat in the back room eating dinner, and after clearing places at the table a woman invited us back to eat. The women began serving a feast of turkey, mutton ribs, and Zuni bread. As we finished, a Zuni man ran in. "Hurry!" he said. "The Shalako are coming!"

Terry took a last bite of pumpkin pie, and I ran outside. The procession was passing in front of the plaza. Racing ahead, I climbed a wall to watch. A Shalako shuffled by with a long, clacking snout and protruding eyes. Downy plumes swayed from the tips of turquoise horns, and eagle feathers burst from the crown; a thick ruff of raven feathers circled the neck, and long black hair fell over a white cloak. Kiva members escorted the Shalako, singing songs of welcome. Other Zuni crowded one side of the street, reaching out to touch the passing kachinas. A few children held back, peering with wide-eyed faces as the procession surged ahead making its grand entrance.

About two o'clock in the morning, the Shalakos began dancing in the newly built homes of sponsoring families. Weaving through the crowd of onlookers, I pressed into the back room of one house. A partition wall, with large openings for viewing, divided the interior in half. Visitors watched from the back; relatives, mainly women and children, sat on folding chairs up front.

Brightly colored shawls and Pendleton blankets hung from the walls. Turquoise necklaces dangled from the necks of mounted deer heads, overlooking the dancers. The ceremony unfolded before a wooden altar, painted in white, black, and turquoise. Offerings of prayer feathers, stone fetishes, and large ceremonial arrowheads lay on a smooth bed of sand in front. More than a century ago, anthropologist Frank Cushing described the Zuni altars as "the border-land wherein the souls of men may approach the spirits of the gods."

The Shalako danced back and forth following a path marked

by white prayer meal. The tall kachina kept within a shallow trench, cut in the dirt floor, to keep its head from scraping the ceiling. Sacred clowns, the mudhead kachinas, worked in pairs to playfully harass the sacred messenger. Nearby, a group of singers sat in a circle facing each other, drumming and shaking gourd rattles. The repetitive dancing and singing lulled the senses, allowing the mind to wander.

While following the dance circuit, we stopped for awhile at the house of the Long Horn, Sayatasha, leader of the council of the gods. According to the Zuni, each person carries within themselves a life road, a breathway. They refer to their deities as the "makers of the trails of our lives." Nearing the end of an all-night recitation, Long Horn prays,

> "May you be blessed with light;
> May your roads be fulfilled . . ."

Reaching the Corn Kiva house, we watched as a Shalako chased the mudheads and clacked his beak in the faces of spectators who dozed off. The kachina worked hard to wake an old woman who had fallen into a deep sleep. Finally her head jerked up with a startled expression as the onlookers laughed. But the Shalako returned to the far side of the room and danced back with an offering of food for her.

Attending the ceremony as observers put us in an ambiguous role. Shalako was a time to act with clear purpose, to participate, to accept without questioning, to be content with the knowledge you are entitled to receive and no more. But this year they tolerated the presence of outsiders, hoping we brought with us good thoughts.

As the sky lightened near dawn, the pace and intensity of the singing increased. The Shalako and mudheads danced with renewed force as the end approached. "Did you notice that?" Terry asked. "It just changed from night to day."

A moment later, the first patch of sunlight struck the inner wall, bringing an end to the dancing.

Now, late in the day, Milzer and I angle up the mesa on the trail to the Stone Lions. At the visitor center I asked the park ranger, a Pueblo Indian, if the trail was prehistoric. "It was always here," he said. "The Park Service just fixed it up."

Below us lie the ruins of ceremonial chambers and living quarters, abandoned about 1550. They had been carved into the cliffs along a two-mile front. On the canyon floor stand the concentric walls of an excavated village, built by Anasazi immigrants from the "great house" pueblos farther west. We have reached the farthest point of our trip around the Four Corners, bending with the elliptic.

Crossing the portreo, the two of us dip in and out of Lummis Canyon. On the rim of the next gorge, we dump our packs. As we set up a tent, I let Milzer know I'm going on. If the snow comes, we'll be forced to return to the road in the morning. This may be the only chance to reach the shrine.

"It'll be dark in less than an hour," he says, studying my reaction. When he realizes I'm serious about continuing, he grabs a water bottle and a flashlight without comment.

Descending 500 feet into Alamo Canyon, we trail past a series of tent rocks. These conical forms have eroded from the bedrock tuff, a volcanic deposit formed in a massive eruption of superheated ash. Twilight settles in the canyon pocket, filling the hollows, flattening the perspective. As we leave the bottom, Milzer estimates we have one more haul to reach the top. He has been timing the distance covered by "hauls." That's the time it takes to haul in a seine net on his fishing boat, about twenty to twenty-five minutes. We ascend the trail up the far wall and onto the mesatop, passing a mound of stone rubble, the ruins of Yapashi, a crescent-shape pueblo.

Night thickens as we approach the shrine, enclosed by a circle of upright stone slabs. An opening to the southeast faces the direction of the winter sunrise. Within the enclosure a circle of interlocked deer antlers glows lunar white in the fading light, ring within ring. At the center crouch a pair of mountain lions, tensed to spring. A lion skull has been placed between the bedrock carvings, among offerings of beads, potsherds, and two deer skulls.

"On the next mesa over," Milzer says, "is the greatest concentration of computer power in the world. People on this one still pray to skulls."

Set so close to the prehistoric ruins, the mountain lions likely pre-date the arrival of the Spanish. But members of Cochiti

Pueblo maintain the sacred enclosure, and other Puebloans continue to leave offerings here. The life-size mountain lions, one male and one female, are carved in bas-relief from an outcrop of volcanic tuff, weather-roughened. The shaped forms represent the Hunter God of the North, a guardian spirit, and his sister the life-giving Mother of Game. The Stone Lions form a point of balance, pairing male with female, the hunt with fertility, death with birth.

A pale moon rises behind a drift of clouds. The ground within the ritual enclosure lies untracked, recently swept clean. This is not the archaeological site I expected but a living shrine, growing more numinous as the light fails. I look around to see who might be nearby but find no one. The place lies vacant. Submerged in the stillness at the end of day, I stand on the edge of the stone circle. No traditions connect me to this place, no blood ties. The only shrine I can claim lies buried deep in the human heart.

Coming to Bandelier was accidental; the weather kept pushing us off-course. But it has brought me to the right place for a story, the one I first set out to tell.

Under the Rim

Years had come and gone since I first stood on the North Rim of the Grand Canyon. A great emptiness opened within. Before me, solid rock disappeared and the sky poured into the gap. I turned away as birds spiraled downward in visceral twists, pulling my thoughts with them.

A rough road brought me to the end of Point Sublime, a promontory reaching into the aerial expanse. Gorges on each side dropped thousands of vertical feet without warning. Rim-rock shifted abruptly from the horizontal to the vertical, from life to death. Below, the rim opened an angular world of edges and boundaries, all or nothing.

Shouldering a pack thrown together with little thought, I worked my way to the west, looking for a break in the arc of cliffs. No trail led to where I was going. I walked hatless under a late afternoon sun, feeling the weight of the heat even at 7,000 feet. It was mid-August, the wrong season for a canyon trek. But something remained unfinished.

Locating a way through the upper cliff, I dropped beneath the high plateau into another realm, older and deeper. The eye led, descending into the lower reaches, and the feet followed. Steep talus covered the stacked cliffs; brush covered the talus. The ground, turned on end, had lost its firmness. The footing shifted and slid with each step. A dislodged rock tumbled far below. I moved unsteadily with the awkwardness of someone who has been away from the canyon for too long. I needed a couple of days to get back into the rhythm of it and adjust to the heat, but there wasn't time.

In this section of the Grand Canyon, farther west than the classic viewpoints, the two rims faced each other across a distance of seven miles and a depth of almost a mile. A saddle connected the rim with Sagittarius Ridge, 1,500 feet below. Halfway to the divide, I sank into the shade of a boulder, exhausted. My original plan was to hike this route in the fall with a couple of my brother's friends, but I had acted on impulse and taken off in the heat of summer. There was no sense to it. Not fully recovered from a recent illness, I felt weaker and more dehydrated than I'd expected. The time had come to turn back, but the thought of a hard scramble up to the rim stalled me.

Looking to the north, I recognized the Holy Grail Temple, a distant landmark above Merlin Abyss. The terrain had a familiar pattern to it, one my brother and I had learned first-hand on the canyon traverse fourteen years before. But the place no longer held my interest. Too tired to go back, I decided to continue to the saddle and wait until morning before returning. Sidestepping down the slope, I made for the dividing ridge.

Red marked the transit into night, a dry red. The sky and the rock — even the shadows turned red as the day ended. Redrock massed to the west, forming the perpendicular walls of the ridge, named for the sky archer. Only the slightest breeze eddied across the top of the saddle. I stretched out among shattered boulders that had fallen from the higher cliffs, unable to fall asleep. Heat radiated from the rock.

The year before, I flew with my brother over this maze of canyons. He had returned to flying after working as a smoke-jumper for a few seasons. His decision to fly again, he said, came after parachuting into a forest fire in Idaho. Running low on food, his crew had hiked out to a landing zone for resupply. John crouched low, holding his hat, as the chopper hovered above him, kicking up sand and throwing gravel. "What am I doing here?" he wondered. "I'm a pilot. I should be up there, not down here eating dust."

On our cross-canyon flight, we turned at Point Sublime and flew between an immense butte named Mencius Temple and the ramparts of Sagittarius. A couple of months later, on a clear June morning, my brother died in a midair collision in this corridor. Death suddenly cracked the pattern, and the sky rushed in.

Friends and family gathered for a wake at his home in the forest south of the canyon. The crowd kept growing as the scattered community converged from throughout the West. Everyone fumbled for a way to reconnect with life, to make sense of something with no sense to it, to find the point of balance. Those who had stopped speaking to each other put aside their differences; those who had lived together for years drew closer. Emotions switched from sorrow to anger and back again. A few people laughed; most cried. A few cried until the only thing left to do was laugh.

After the wake, we reassembled on the South Rim for a memorial service in the open air. Death had taken us by surprise, and no one knew how to go about these things. All we could do was act in a way that stayed true to the life suddenly ended. One by one, those closest to my brother came forward to tell their stories. Finally Jones Benally, a Navajo friend of his, walked to the rim to speak. He wore his hair knotted at the back of the neck beneath a cowboy hat. A turquoise-and-shell necklace draped down his chest, and a bowguard covered his left wrist.

"The person you miss will never return," he began. Jones had trained as a singer for a number of years and now spoke with force, his voice directed at the living. "But you have to be strong. When I was a boy they tell me two things: You have to be strong, and no matter what happens you got to carry on. When we die, that's the other side of the curtain. Both spirits are together in us. The bad spirit is only one that hangs around, the one they call ghost. The good spirit never changes, is never old, nothing. Our body goes back, belongs to earth."

Jones paused a moment as a breeze lifted a prayer feather, dangling from a piñon branch. And then he cried out, "Nobody lives forever!"

When he had finished, my brother's young son and daughter walked to the cliff edge, each holding a flower. Standing together, they tossed their flowers into the canyon and turned back. I stayed on the rim a while longer until only a flatness remained, a distance turned inward.

Rubble from decomposed cliffs filled the saddle where I was now camped. From above, these massive sandstone blocks had appeared insignificant. But when I dropped below the rim, the perspective shifted. The canyon's immense scale absorbed the human presence, leaving a place where people disappear altogether.

Point Sublime faded back into the wall of the plateau as the final light fell. More than a century ago, the panoramic view from the promontory drew Clarence Dutton. The geologist gazed into the depths, finding the magnitude so overwhelming he was conscious only of "a troubled sense of immensity."

At dawn the outer rim emerged from the dark matrix. I was already awake and rested, feeling stronger than yesterday and no longer certain about the need to turn back. Faced with having to leave before completing what I had come to do, I hesitated.

As the sky lightened, I could see deep into the canyon and across the Tonto, a sunken terrace bordering the deepest gorge. Somewhere out there, miles away, was the crash site. Going fast and light, I thought, and hiking through the heat of day might give me a chance. Once on the broad Tonto, 2,500 feet lower, I'd be exposed to the full force of the sun. But I needed to reach the crash site. A long day, a hard push, and it would be done.

Shadows began drawing back into the deeper clefts of rock. If I was going to do it, I had to go now. Packing a little food and a water bottle, I took off, leaving behind the rest of the gear. If all went well, I'd be back by dark.

Rockfall fanned out below the saddle in an apron of talus, angling steeply down to the lip of the Redwall. I picked my way through the breakdown for 1,000 feet, searching for secure footing but rarely finding it. Erosion had undercut an immense boulder that rested precariously on loose fill. I eased past the balanced rock in boots stained red by the dust. No rain had fallen for a long time.

The Redwall brought me to a stop. Nothing looked familiar. Sheer cliffs fell away in a curving wall of red-streaked limestone. Finding a way through looked impossible, but I knew it could be

done since I'd climbed it before without a rope. I studied a spur
ridge, roughened by ledges. That had to be the route. Weather-
eaten into sharp points, the rock snagged hands and clothes as I
hugged close to it. Stretching for footholds on one pitch, scrambling on another, I downclimbed to the base of the cliff.

Once in the bed of the tributary gorge, the walking became
easier. Route finding was now straightforward, leaving me to my
own thoughts. I moved quickly, trying to cover as much ground
as possible before the sun edged overhead. Far above, a redtail
hawk tipped a wing, curving into the blue.

My brother once described the exhilaration of flying with a
redtail. At the time, he was carrying a party of river runners out
of the canyon by helicopter. Catching a thermal for added lift,
he glanced to his left and spotted the hawk flying close enough
to make eye contact. Rising on the stream of heated air, the redtail kept glancing his way. It showed no fear, only curiosity. The
two of them flew together, climbing higher until they topped the
rim and went their separate ways.

I followed the northwest arm of Tuna Creek, a Spanish bor-
rowing of an Indian name for the fruit of the prickly pear cactus. A clump of green grew from the bed, screening an oily seep,
almost dry. It was probably okay to drink, but I didn't have time
to soak it up with my shirt and wring it into a cup.

Nearing the junction with the main gorge, the walls spread
farther apart and the sun poured in. As I crossed the shadow-
line into bright light, the air switched abruptly from cool to hot.
Reaching the entrenched bed of Tuna, I turned up-canyon. A
break opened in the opposite wall leading onto the Tonto Plateau. Aiming for it, I passed a pothole, worn in the bedrock. It
held a couple of gallons of water. With half a quart left, I passed
it by, planning to fill up here on my return.

Leaving the dry creekbed, I angled up the sandstone cliff to an
even drier Tonto. The plateau appeared level from a distance, but
on foot the surface rolled into ridges and dropped into ravines.
Talus rested in long, sweeping curves at the foot of each cliff.

By late morning the heat had grown intense. Unaccountably
I'd left my hat behind. Rationing what little water remained,
I ignored my thirst and pressed on with only a rough idea of
where to find the crash site. The helicopter had fallen somewhere

along the margin of the plateau, notched by gorges. These obstacles deflected me from a straight-line course. Being forced to detour across the heads of the drainages added to the distance. My route meandered over the terrace, dodging blackbrush, cactus, and ravine. I veered to the edge of the main gorge a few times to check for the crash site, but without luck. Throughout the morning I kept up a steady pace, unwilling to lose time by stopping to rest.

Hard light filled the canyon, grinding the redrock to dull hues and fusing the sky solid. Nothing else moved as I walked through the stillness. Soon out of water, I felt the heat take its toll, pressing down with a dead weight. Thoughts evaporated, the blood thickened, the feet grew heavy.

And all the time I realized what was happening. Having hiked in the canyon hundreds of times, I knew what was possible. But whenever I told myself to turn back, I overrode my better judgment and continued. I knew the danger but pushed on despite the risk, compelled by reasons unclear even to me.

Arms folded, I walked with my eyes to the ground, mesmerized by one foot swinging before the other. I followed the path of least resistance, avoiding the roughest terrain, trying to conserve strength. I kept walking, unsure if I'd ever find the site.

Suddenly the hairs on my neck prickled, and I knew for certain I had found it. But a quick check of the immediate surroundings turned up nothing. Then, crossing the ridgetop, I noticed a pair of long indentations in the sand. They were tracks from the skids of a helicopter, left by one of the search teams. I looked toward the edge of the inner gorge and saw a black swath of charred rock and brush, roughly matching the outline of a helicopter. This was it. Two months after the accident, a burnt scent still hung in the air.

Teams from the Park Service, sheriff's office, and National Transportation Safety Board had combed the scene of the crash for a week. They retrieved the bodies of the twenty-five victims and searched for bits of wreckage, looking for clues to understand how the accident had occurred. After finishing their investigation, they removed most of the wreckage.

But pieces of the metal fuselage, melted by the intense fire, lay mixed with shards of tinted Plexiglas, a broken seat buckle, the cracked eyepiece from a pair of binoculars. I glanced over the scattered debris left in the wake of death, trying to find something to help make sense of it. I found nothing.

The full heat of the desert pressed down. The sun perched directly overhead, noon high. I now faced the return hike in the afternoon heat, already exhausted. I felt light-headed and needed to find water soon. Quickly I built a cairn to mark the site, piling stone upon stone, burning my hands with each rock I picked up. The ground was superheated, hotter than I wanted to think about. The air temperature must have been well above 100 degrees, measured in the shade, and climbing. But there wasn't any shade. To protect my burned fingers, I carried the dark rocks between the palms of my hand.

Placing the last stone on the cairn, I stood for a moment and said a prayer for my brother and those who had died with him. It ended with a few words learned from a hitchhiker long ago. "From where the sun rises, to where the sun sets . . ."

The air held still, so unmoving a faint sound could be heard lifting from deep within the gorge. I listened a moment to the faraway flow of the river and turned back.

Head bent under the sun, I retraced my steps. Sunlight pounded the expanse, hammering thin all color and depth. My pace soon faltered as the dryness worked its way from mouth to throat, and then deeper. I had pushed too hard, misjudged the distance, ignored the heat. Angry at myself for having been so reckless, I kept going.

Within an hour after leaving the crash site, my scalp began to tingle and my stomach clenched, beginning to cramp. A shimmering darkness narrowed my visual field, closing in around the edge of sight. This was serious, and happening too fast to understand. Symptoms of extreme dehydration, I thought, shouldn't have appeared for another day. I expected thirst and exhaustion, but not this.

I stumbled along, having to will my feet high enough to clear the ground. Needles from prickly pear cactus pierced my light boots and worked their way into my feet. At first I extracted the longer spines, but soon gave up the effort and left them in.

Sunlight penetrated the lens of air, boring down with a manic intensity. I searched for shade of any kind, but couldn't find a boulder large enough to throw a shadow. The sun stood straight up. I slumped down and curled around a blackbrush, pressing into the spiky branches without finding any shade. Struggling up again, I kept going.

Heat radiated from the ground as the temperature climbed. My body felt light and floating but moved in slow motion, one step after another. Every few minutes I stopped but couldn't rest. The act of sitting down and standing up took more energy than it gained. Covering the plateau, tufts of vegetation bristled from the ground like a mineral encrustation. When I crossed this stretch of canyon the last time, more than a dozen years ago, mud was ankle deep and every wash flowed.

Somewhere across the broken expanse was the waterpocket I'd passed earlier. But after all the walking, the perspective remained unchanged, the distance held. I felt no closer as my chance of reaching it slipped away. For the first time I knew I might die. And the realization came without surprise. The choice of living or dying no longer held much interest for me. And then I thought of my wife and son. They couldn't go through another death so soon, it would be too much. Knowing I had to live, I pushed on.

When the body becomes seriously dehydrated, judgment also evaporates. Simple decisions become difficult. As my thoughts dried up, I began to veer off-course, losing the thread, choosing the harder way. At one point I paused on a steep shoulder and glanced at the ridge above, where I should have been walking.

Then I saw it. On the slope lay a piece of wreckage overlooked by the search parties. They hadn't expected to find anything this far north. It was the missing rotor blade from my brother's helicopter, scarred from the impact of metal on metal. Later retrieved, it turned out to be a critical piece of evidence used in reconstructing the moment of collision. In the final instant, it's likely neither aircraft could have seen the other as the airplane overtook the helicopter from above and behind. All I could do at the time was map the location of the debris and continue.

Submerged in rock and sky, I walked for so long that even the reason for walking burned away. The sun flared overhead as light swept down, wave after wave, until all that remained was shimmering heat. Contouring above a drop-off, I angled toward the head of a dry ravine. The ledgerock led to a notch. Descending through the breach in the cliff, I noticed a narrow band of shadow where the rim had been undercut. It held the only piece of shade for miles.

Wanting to go on to water, I couldn't. I had lost momentum. The bone-dry air, the heat, the utter tiredness left me no choice. Pulling myself partway beneath the overhang, I lay dust-still. The low overhang left only a foot of clearance above, but it was enough.

An airplane soon passed overhead, flying above the rim. My only hope was to make a signal fire. I fumbled for a lighter, ready to torch the nearest clump of brush if it returned.

Sometime later I heard the drone of an approaching plane, but a deep inertia had set in. I lacked the strength to crawl to the nearest bush, ten feet away. The sound of the airplane faded off, leaving only a stillness in its wake. All I could do was shade-up until the sun dropped below the rim of Sagittarius. In the cool of the evening I might have a chance to reach the waterpocket, a mile and a half away. So close.

Conserving every trace of moisture became essential; I kept my mouth shut, breathing through my nose to reduce the loss. I lay still, resisting the impulse to take any action. At the same time I was afraid that by doing nothing, I would die. As dehydration progressed, I might become too weak to cover the distance still ahead.

But less than an hour after taking shelter, I began to recover. No much, but enough to wedge my entire body under the rock. Getting out of the sun had reduced the heat load, making a difference. Heat was a critical factor, but finding water consumed my thinking. Without it, I was continuing to dehydrate even in the shade. Having regained some strength, my resolve to wait until sundown weakened. I began thinking about the possibility of trying to reach the waterpocket. Maybe I'd have a chance if a cloud moved in.

With that thought, I began to hallucinate. It might have saved my life. Next to me sat an old Indian, unsmiling. One moment he was simply there, appearing so naturally his presence didn't startle me. His black hair hung loose, framing a broad face and spilling over the shoulders of a cotton tunic. His style of clothing placed him in the last century and his facial features appeared to be Apache, but I wasn't certain. If so, the old man was a long way from home.

"Yes, we wait here, sun go down," he told me, lifting his chin toward the far cliff. "Then go to water." The words came from deep in his throat, spoken with a simple kindness. What the old man said only confirmed what I knew to be necessary. But confirmation was what I needed. To have pushed on in the heat would have been lethal.

Dehydration had shaken my body's biochemical balance, activating the appearance of the old man. But it happened without a sense of disorientation, allowing me to consider what was taking place. While accurate in detail and dimension, the form of the man next to me lacked physical heft; it was without substance. But the image wasn't ghostly, and if a vision, it didn't generate a sense of deep significance. His extraordinary presence unfolded in a matter-of-fact way, as if I had stepped outside a dream and looked back.

In a world of appearances, we live as if reality lies just beneath the surface, somewhere beyond the reach of the senses. But peel away the layers of appearance and all we're left with is pure event. Whatever the origin, the old man represented something more than a symptom. I didn't talk to him, but I did listen.

He kept me company for about fifteen minutes before leaving. By then, I had recovered enough to shift to the wider end of the overhang where I sat hunched over, waiting for the sun to go down. The dark rock framed the opening like the eye of a mask. Beyond it, light poured into the rift between the canyon walls, catching on the fractured angles of rock. Removing my boots, I picked out the cactus needles.

Five hours after I crawled into the overhang, the sun set. When it happened, it happened fast. The sun balanced on the raw edge of Sagittarius, flaring upward as if the rock itself had caught fire. Then it was gone, leaving only the highest cliffs in full light. I fumbled to pull on my boots, needing to take full advantage of whatever ambient light remained. With apprehension, I set out.

Moving cautiously to test my strength, I crossed the wash and threaded my way up the far side of the ravine. I worked from ledge to ledge, feeling weak but not unsteady. Once on the terrace above, I maintained an even pace, slowly covering ground. With only indirect light, the canyon became transformed as cliff walls dissolved in a burning incandescence. The rock glowed red as it emitted heat absorbed during the day. A wash of pale light spread above the rims, and darkness welled up from the inner gorge.

An hour later I reached the floor of the main drainage. In the past, flash floods had scoured the channel down to bedrock, scooping out shallow pockets where water sometimes collected. Only one of these had lasted through the summer heat, the one I now approached.

Just below me, the pool opened skyward, reflecting the last light. The thrill of nearing water grew difficult to contain; I had to check the impulse to fling myself into it. At this moment, more than any other, I realized the necessity to act purposely. What it meant to be human, what it meant to be alive was somehow contained in how I took this first drink of water.

Carefully removing my pack, I offered a few words of thanks for the beauty of the world and the life it gives. Then I knelt down and filled a metal cup with the liquid. Each motion flowed with conscious intent. I took a sip and continued drinking until it was drained. Two more cupfuls followed without any release. The thirst had gone too deep to quench.

Night came, filling the gorge and erasing the distinction between cliff and slope. Unable to go farther, I climbed into an overhang where my brother and I had camped on our long canyon traverse years ago. With my gear still cached miles above, I found a spot to bivouac for the night and scooped shallow indentations for my hip and shoulder. My only food was a piece of tortilla but my mouth was too dry to swallow it. Mixed with a little water it turned soft, but I still couldn't swallow. My throat was too parched.

The sky above the rim held a trace of light, lasting long after the sun had set. I watched it withdraw to the west, thinking about the hike out. No matter what difficulties lay ahead, I was no longer worried. The trajectory had curved back on itself. In a time of loss, I had lost sight of the need to be alive and had stumbled into circumstances where the choice became very clear. Finally at peace, I stretched out, covered only by the stars. Nothing more.

The night sky darkened, and the eye reached deeper. Stars emerged from the dark to flood the sky with enough light to cast a shadow. Stars kept appearing until their brightness covered the known constellations. New patterns emerged. At night the sky lies wide open, spreading into endless space. Nothing is hidden. Nothing more can be given. It all lies open before us.

Deep in the night, I rolled over trying to get warm, drawing my knees up. In the desert air, the heat of day quickly dissipates. Rolling over again and tucking my hands between my legs, I remembered the stash of firewood.

Checking the backwall of the overhang, I found a few pieces of wood placed there long ago, the ones my brother had left behind for someone who might need them. Lighting a small fire, I curled around the warmth and watched the flames pulse and flicker. In the end, all we are left with are the big questions and the small kindnesses. The rest falls away.

Night has overtaken us in the backcountry of Bandelier. Clouds tumble over the Jemez Mountains, covering the moon. The next storm threatens. Leaving the Shrine of the Stone Lions, Scott Milzer and I return the way we came. We take the trail leading back across the plateau and past the ruins of Yapashi, now buried under a midden of dark sky.

Tree branches interlock, forming a flat wall in front of us and hiding the pathway. We take out our flashlights. I shake mine trying to get it to work. Nothing. Batteries must be dead. I glance at the cloudcover, seeing a thin spot.

"Maybe we'll have some moonlight."

"We're not going to have shit," Milzer says. "We're going to be on our hands and knees any moment, feeling for boot tracks in the trail."

He takes the lead as I try to follow his faint beam. The depth of field has shrunk to a few feet. A trail sign warns us of washouts ahead, hazardous to foot travel. We reach the rim of Alamo Canyon where the cliffs fall away, disappearing into a deep rift. And keep going.

As we start down, Milzer clicks off his light so our eyes can adjust. We descend the cliff face, letting our feet find their way down the switchbacks. The dark presses in, dissolving the surfaces and transforming the surroundings. At night the rock flows, closing in when we stop, parting when we walk. We descend deeper into the gorge, never recognizing the bottom until we begin to ascend.

Stairs, carved in the cliffrock, climb the opposite wall in winding flights known as the Grand Staircase. A hole opens in the cloud cover as Milzer tops the rim, silhouetted against the moon. We leave the trail and weave through the scattered trees, reaching camp where the piñons stand blue under a lunar sky.

Rolling out before sunrise, I fire up the stove and put on a pot of water. The weather-edge of the storm has stalled just west of Bandelier, giving us a brief reprieve. Something stirs on the eastern skyline, a slight shift in density. Dawn begins to arch above the horizon in a pale swell, light traveling outward toward no particular destination. I watch it, breathing in the morning air, cold and clear.

Each trip finds its own end. Our route has taken us across the edge of winter, through high deserts and into deep canyons, past the home of Little Boy and Fat Man. Reaching Bandelier has brought with it a sense of completion, a sense of having rounded the outer curve of the ellipse. All that remains is Burntwater. Most of what I know about the place comes from a Navajo who grew up nearby.

"Burntwater," said Sammy M. James. He wore a slab of turquoise dangling from an ear and a Four Corners Power Plant cap on his head. "I once asked my grandfather how it got that name, Tsól déélid.

"Way back when, there was a well there." He motioned with his arm to indicate a circular pool of water. "They say an old man lived about two blocks away. People from all around came to it. There's not much water in that dry country. It was winter and the water froze."

Where water surfaces in the desert, the center of gravity shifts. Trails converge, the lines of force intersect. And even in the desert, water can turn to ice.

"The old man built a fire all the way around it," he added. "It worked." A circle of fire burned in the high desert and the water flowed.

Some Navajo women weave a style of rug known as the Burntwater pattern. The more traditional weavers leave a slight imperfection in the rug design, usually a single strand of yarn crossing the border from the interior to the outer edge. Traders say it's a spirit path; anthropologists call it a ceremonial break. To the casual eye it may appear to be a flaw, but the weaver places it there intentionally. A Navajo woman told me it was to keep her thoughts from being trapped in the pattern. A woman weaves only one perfect rug in her lifetime, her last. A weaving needs a break in the pattern; a map needs a blank spot.

Milzer wakes up and reminds me he has a plane to catch. Time to head back to Flagstaff. We pack up before the snow flies and return to the roadhead at a fast pace. Only a few vehicles remain in the parking lot at park headquarters; anticipating the storm, the rest have left.

Descending into the valley, we pass Santa Fe without a pause, hitting Albuquerque and turning west. America's dream of the open road, old Route 66, lies beneath the interstate and reappears at unexpected moments as a cutoff meander curving away on another path. Moving steadily, we thread between pueblo and mesa. Mud tracks streak the pavement at each interchange, feeding in from the deeper country. Snow flies as the highway takes us into another storm.

Below Mount Taylor, the interstate crosses an old lava flow where snow has gathered on rock squeezed from volcanic vents, weathered and worn, crumbled and shattered. Over it the highway flows in smooth hydraulic curves. It transforms the rough terrain into pure motion, letting us move across the surface with the momentum of a rock skipping over water.

Ahead lies the turnoff to Burntwater, but no road sign marks it. I let Milzer know we're approaching the exit. No response. The road map stays tucked behind the visor without either of us reaching for it. Names we place on the land fall away one by one until the map turns blank. For us, Burntwater has turned into pure direction. I pass the turnoff and keep driving. The storm has wiped the slate clean, covering the desert with snow as far as the eye can see.

About the Author

Scott Thybony brings to his writing a background in
anthropology, a zest for remote places, and work as a
Colorado River guide and archaeologist. A graduate
of the University of Arizona, the Flagstaff resident
has lived with indigenous peoples in the American
Southwest and the Canadian Arctic. He writes books
for the National Geographic Society, guidebooks to
historic and natural areas, and collections of essays.
His travels through western North America have
resulted in award-winning articles in *Smithsonian*
and *National Geographic Traveler* and contributions
to national magazines such as *Outside* and
Men's Journal.